Fire of the North

ALSO BY DAVID ADAM

THE EDGE OF GLORY
Prayers in the Celtic Tradition 1985

THE CRY OF THE DEER
Meditations on the Hymn of St Patrick 1987

TIDES AND SEASONS
Modern Prayers in the Celtic Tradition 1989

THE EYE OF THE EAGLE
Meditations on the hymn 'Be thou my vision' 1990

BORDER LANDS
The best of David Adam 1991 (SPCK hardback)

POWER LINES
Celtic Prayers about Work 1992

DAVID ADAM

FIRE
NORTH
of the

An Illustrated Life of St Cuthbert

Photographs and drawings by
Jean Freer

First published 1993

SPCK
Holy Trinity Church
Marylebone Road
London NW1 4DU

British Library Cataloguing in Publication Data
A catalogue record for this book is available from the British Library.

ISBN 0–281–04698–0

Typeset by J&L Composition Ltd, Filey, North Yorkshire
Printed in Great Britain by
Biddles Ltd, Guildford and King's Lynn

To Denise,
and the people of Lindisfarne

Contents

LIST OF PHOTOGRAPHS

Meditation to the Most Blessed Cuthbert

*I would like to know, God's dear saint, what work you
did or what virtue you manifested that pleased Christ
so much . . . I have no doubt that you have some
special quality in regard to which none was found like
you, and it is that quality I propose to investigate.
. . . Open the ear of my understanding that I might
know what it was.*

14TH-CENTURY MONK OF FARNE

For God and for Saint Cuthbert
COLOPHON AT THE END OF THE LINDISFARNE GOSPELS

1

Star-filled Skies

THEY were dark times. War and slaughter were never far away. Only in the last few days news had come that Oswin the ruler of Deira had been murdered by followers of Oswy king of Bernicia. No doubt the call would soon go out to serve king and country. Yet it was good to be sixteen, with all of life ahead of you, full of potential and promise, to be counted as an adult and to be given responsibility. Cuthbert was dreaming along these lines one night, as he watched over a great flock of sheep. There were others with him, older and more experienced, but they were sleeping. It was his turn, on these high moors, to keep awake and to watch, to keep the fire burning and to protect the sheep from harm. A horse neighed and at once he was alert but, recognising the sound as his own mare, he was not too anxious. All the same, his hand grasped his spear in case something happened.

The fire was burning dimly and eyes reflecting its light came closer in out of the darkness. He knew that these eyes belonged to the sheep, but he had to see if there were any other watchers near by. The Leader valley was a place of wild beasts and robbers. Cuthbert strained his eyes and ears to discover if anythinwas moving out there. All his senses were alert. A good way off a startled bird cried. Something, he knew, must be on the move. One thing influences another: if the spider's web trembles, its tremors are felt by the tree, the roots and the very earth. A person who was sensitive enough to the earth would feel those vibrations. Even now, Cuthbert was aware of a bird nearly a mile off. How he wished he was still more sensitive. Silently he prayed that

he might be more open to the Presence that was all around him, more open to the God-given powers that were in him. As was his custom, he prayed with his eyes open, gazing into the starry night.

The dark nights had not long returned, for it was the end of August. The air was warm and the stars shone brightly. It would be a good few hours before the dawn. This thought made Cuthbert look to the south-east. Ever since he was born a strange light had shone out from that direction. He was looking towards the island of Lindisfarne, the home of Saint Aidan. From this tiny place, for sixteen years, Aidan and his monastic followers had reached out into all of Northumbria, especially the hill country of Bernicia. Little cells of monks were springing up all over the place. One such was at Melrose not far from where Cuthbert was watching his sheep. There the great teacher Boisil, second only to Aidan himself, was influencing a whole school of young men. Yet another group of monks and nuns were out at Coldingham, on the cliffs overlooking the sea, the princess Ebba their abbess. Cuthbert knew all this well, for he was one of the small group that had grown up as Christians. He had been well schooled by his foster mother Kenswith, who had been one of the earliest nuns in the whole of the kingdom. Continuing to look south-eastwards, Cuthbert's thoughts were all of Aidan, this heroic monk who was changing the shape and feeling of a whole area. He was a strange man who did not seek to possess anything, but only desired to set people free. If given money, he gave it to the poor, or used it to ransom slaves and set them free. Many of these slaves stayed on at Lindisfarne and went to school there; afterwards some even became the new generation of missionary priests. These men were God-filled adventurers who seemed to fear nothing. They lived the Gospel by their example. They shone like the stars in a dark time.

Whilst Cuthbert mused, the fire burnt low. He had almost let it go out. Carefully he added some dry twigs and thin sticks until the flames flared, seeming to disperse the night. He thought with affection of Kenswith his foster mother and teacher, who was forever saying he was called to be a light in the dark. 'I'll show them,' he suddenly said to himself, and threw a huge log on the fire. Immediately there was a great rising of sparks, higher and higher. Fascinated, he watched them, countless lights in the dark. They seemed to be reaching to the very stars themselves, changing colour and descending. Now he was not quite sure what was going on. The very stars did seem to be descending. Lights were making their way to earth. The whole of the sky towards Lindisfarne and Bebbaburgh was alive with light. Remembering other shepherds on a hillside, he strained his ears to hear the angelic song, but the night was quite still. There was nothing, not even the sound of a bird. Yet something strange was clearly going on, not the Northern Lights, for it was in the wrong direction. The light now seemed to be leaving the earth away to the south-east and rising to heaven. The picture which now came into his mind was that of Jacob's ladder at Bethel. Strange thoughts in the dark. Could it be angels descending and ascending? Perhaps they were communicating with someone, or even taking some holy soul to heaven. As he continued to stare into the night the movement began to die down. Cuthbert needed witnesses. He should have awakened the shepherds earlier, but at least he would do so now. A loud call had them seizing their spears and jumping to their feet, ready for battle. They were not so ready, however, to look at the stars. He was a strange character, this Cuthbert, a bit uncanny to have around. Their sleepy eyes peered in the direction Cuthbert was pointing. They were so heavy with sleep they hardly could see the stars – everything just seemed dark. Cuthbert could not convince them that there was anything there. In fact by now all had settled down to a very ordinary night. Whatever it had been had passed away from the earth.

During this time, things had indeed been happening down at Bebbaburgh, where Aidan had come on one of his preaching missions. He was under the very shadow of the fortress and its great rock when he was taken ill. He lay right up against his little church but they were afraid to move him, as the least movement was causing him distress. So they built a little tent around him to keep off the night air. They would send to the fortress for help, but it was his heart and they feared he would not last much longer. With the aid of a dear friend he was propped up against a wooden buttress on the west side of the church.

He wanted to be able to see Lindisfarne just once more. He mouthed the word, 'Lindisfarne'. Immediately he began to smile, the pain seemed to be fading away. He was heard to say 'Pools of light, pools of light', and a strange brightness came over his face. For a moment the same light seemed to fill the tent and all around it. Aidan the torch bearer had died.

Cuthbert, meanwhile, was distressed at how easily the other shepherds had gone back to sleep. He thought they could have looked into the night for a little longer. People miss so much if they are not alert or if they go through life half asleep. He himself felt so awake and full of energy. 'O what wretches we are', he mused. 'We are so dull and full of sleep that we miss the Glory that is all about us. If only we could open our eyes. Even tonight whilst watching and praying, I have seen great wonders from God. Tonight surely some holy person has entered into the bright realms of light. Yet here we struggle on in the dark.'

LIGHTEN OUR DARKNESS

Lighten our darkness
We beseech you, O Lord.

Lord, open our eyes
That we may see your Glory.

Lord, open our ears
That we may hear your call.

Lord, open our minds
That we may know your mysteries.

Lord, open our hearts
That they may vibrate with your love.

Lord, make us alert to you
That we may discover your presence.

Lord, make us sensitive to you
That we may learn your purpose.

Lighten our darkness
We beseech you, O Lord.

2

The Life that Vibrates

WHEN the news reached the shepherds that Aidan had died on that same day, it sent a shiver down Cuthbert's spine. For a brief moment he felt icy cold and experienced a twinge of fear. Once again he knew he was in the grip of something far bigger than himself. He did not like to talk much about it, because most people would not understand. When he looked back, there were certain events in his life that defied a simple explanation or at least had a feeling of mystery about them. Kenswith, to whom he had confided them all had simply replied, 'Pools of light, pools of light'.

Now Cuthbert wanted to be alone. He wanted to find himself a desert place. He needed time to think and to pray. This was not a day for him to be with the shepherds. Fortunately, they were sleepy as usual. The routine of working at night called for sleep in the daytime. But for Cuthbert today could not be a day of sleep; too many strings were being plucked in his mind. His whole life was vibrating with a strange call. Throughout the rest of his life the same process would be at work, like the rhythm of the tides around Lindisfarne. He loved being with people and in the thick of things, then suddenly he needed to be away and by himself. Now he needed to be alone. He quietly left for the hills and a favourite cave.

Even as he climbed the hill, his mind went back to the time when he was only eight. He remembered he was often the leader of the little group of lads, how agile and strong he was. Once there had been a group of them, after having a swim, doing acrobatics on the green, whilst still stark naked. A little child of only three began to scream and

wail. The poor mite seemed heart-broken. Cuthbert, with his usual concern, stopped what he was doing and asked the child what was the matter. *'You* are the matter, Cuthbert', wailed the child with great heaving sobs.

'Why, what have I done?'

The child continued to weep and sobbed, 'O holy bishop and priest Cuthbert, these sorts of games are not right for one of your high calling.'

The words frightened Cuthbert, for the voice sounded like an adult's and these were no words for a child. It sent a shiver down his spine. Yet he could not understand what the child was saying. To comfort the child he left the field properly dressed and made for home. Kenswith only smiled when he asked her what it meant. She closed her eyes and, for the first time that he could remember, said, 'Pools of light, pools of light'. At the very thought of this, Cuthbert felt the same tremor run through him. There was a strange pattern unfolding.

He sat down on a rock among the browning heather, his hands on his knees. The next memory came flooding back. It had happened the same year as the incident with the child. Suddenly his agility and well being had been taken from him. He had a severe swelling of the knee and his sinews contracted. His leg was extremely painful and he could not put his foot to the ground. He was so lame that he had to be carried outside and propped against a wall to be in the warmth of the sun. Cuthbert wondered sadly whether he would ever walk again. The day was blazing hot. In the far distance he watched the light shimmer and quake in the heat. Something quite insubstantial was coming towards him. But as he watched, it took shape, in fact the very solid shape of a man on horseback. The man was of a bright appearance, dressed in white, and his face was amazingly beautiful. He greeted Cuthbert with words of blessing. 'God's peace and wholeness be upon you.' Cuthbert, unable to rise, felt ill at ease. 'Forgive me, noble sir. If I was not lame on account of my sin, I would rise and wait on so gracious a guest.' At these words the man descended from his horse and examined Cuthbert's knee. He gave Cuthbert these instructions. 'Cook a pan of wheat flour in milk, until the wheat becomes a soft paste. Then put the paste on your knee whilst it is still hot.' Then he mounted his magnificently caparisoned horse and rode away. Cuthbert watched until the shape seemed to break down in the distant heat haze and become pools of light. He lay there wondering if he had dreamt it. By the time his friends came for him he was certain that he had seen an angel. In relating this to Kenswith he only got a knowing smile. Soon he was yelping like a little pup as Kenswith put a hot wheat poultice on his knee, as had been prescribed. It was so pure and white, Cuthbert knew it would draw the poison out. In a few days, as promised, he was cured. Now on the moorside, Cuthbert hugged his knee and smiled. He had seen an angel. His would be a life that was never denied the help of angels. With this strange thought he set off again.

Now he came within sight of a shepherd's little bothy. The thatch looked as if it had fallen in. Immediately his mind went back to his first campaign with the Bernician army. They had been making their own way home from the far end of the kingdom. He had become separated from the others and was approaching the River Wear. By now the rain was icy, and being driven with great force. He felt weak and needed shelter. The whole area was deserted. There was no one who could help him or sustain horse and rider for the journey. So he unsaddled his horse and led it to a bothy, just like the little hut he could see now. He remembered well how he had tied the horse to the wall inside the hut, and waited for the storm to cease. He had hardly started to pray, when the horse raised its head to the roof of the hut and, grabbing part of the thatch, pulled it towards him. Immediately, from somewhere above, out fell a parcel in a linen cloth. When Cuthbert had finished his prayers he opened the linen cloth and discovered inside it fresh bread and meat. He thanked God for providing food in the wilderness, and shared the bread with his horse. After eating he set out again in the strength of this food. He knew that when he prayed strange things happened; if he did not pray they did not seem to happen.

Even this thought triggered off yet another memory. He was on the north side of the great river, the Tyne. Not far from the mouth of the river, on the opposite side, was a monastery. Some of the monks were ferrying wood on rafts to use at the monastery. Suddenly, out of the west came a violent wind. The rafts and monks were being swept downriver towards the sea. Some of the brothers, seeing this, launched out in little boats to help those that were struggling with the rafts, but they were forced back by the violence of the winds and the increasingly strong current. The monks with their rafts were now in real danger of being swept out to sea. They were beyond human help. People began to gather around to watch the drama. Five monks, like little birds in the water, were being swept away, each on his own raft, not even able to help each other. 'God help them,' muttered a bystander. 'Rubbish to that,' chimed in another. 'Let them perish,' said the crowd. Cuthbert was appalled and tried to stop their curses. But they merely became angry with him, 'Let no one pray for them, and may God have no mercy on any of them. They have robbed us of our old ways of worship. The troubles we have surely are due to this.'

Cuthbert made no reply but watched and waited. Suddenly he felt the time was right and knelt down in their midst. He bowed his head until it touched the ground and prayed. Immediately the wind turned around and the little rafts were driven to the very place they wanted to be. Sounds of rejoicing arose from the far bank. The country folk were overawed, and did not know what to say to Cuthbert as he arose. They were ashamed of their unbelief and promised to respect the God who did such wonderful things. Cuthbert himself was glad that he understood the elements and that God did answer his prayer.

Throughout the day, as Cuthbert stood in the cave looking over the hills, these events and others passed before him. Kenswith's mysterious words would not leave his mind: 'Pools of light, pools of light'. He knew that something of great magnitude was happening to him. He knew it was linked with Aidan and the island of Lindisfarne. But beyond that he was not sure.

> *Lord, let not the clouds hide your Glory.*
> *Glory at the heart of Creation,*
> *Glory at the centre of the Universe,*
> *Glory in the deepest depths of matter,*
> *Glory in each of the elements,*
> *Glory in each strand of the web of life,*
> *Glory in each connection, though it be*
> *As thin as a gossamer thread,*
> *Or thick as a rope of iron.*
> *Glory in the very depth of our being.*
> *Lord, let not the clouds hide your Glory.*
> *You are there waiting to be revealed.*
> *Glory in each object and each creature,*
> *Glory in each life and every encounter,*
> *Glory in our past, and waiting in our future.*
> *Make us sensitive to your Presence and your call.*
> *Lord, let not the clouds hide your Glory.*

3

Melrose

CUTHBERT did not know which way to turn. He thought of visiting Kenswith or of going to Lindisfarne – both were easy journeys. He was not sure anyone would understand what was calling him out from following the sheep. He was sure it was not a 'what' but 'Who'. This was not the fates, or destiny, this was a personal call from a personal God. Cuthbert was sure that being a person mattered. Who you are influences what you say – it speaks louder than words. You cannot give yourself to God until you have become someone. This sort of conversation with himself made up his mind. If Aidan had still been alive, Cuthbert would have gone straight to the island of Lindisfarne. He needed no one to convince him that he was being called. With Aidan dead, he would go to Melrose. There were still many holy men who could instruct him by example and in book work on Lindisfarne, but at Melrose was Boisil, a man already famous for his learning and sanctity. Cuthbert made up his mind. Then he realised that, though he sought the kingdom of God, he must first return to his home. Kenswith must be told of his decision and of his whereabouts, or she would have the whole area searched for him.

The journey to the village of Wrangham and Kenswith led along familiar paths. These were roads whose origins were lost in antiquity. He passed a group of standing stones, a former place of worship still visited by some of the local people at their high festivals. There was still much superstition and paganism in Northumbria. Cuthbert signed himself with the sign of the cross and moved on. After a mile or so, he sat on a large flat stone to rest a while. Here, carved into the rock,

were spirals and circles. The whole of the flat surface was covered by them. It reminded him of a prayer that Kenswith had taught him. She had told him of the circular defence around her monastery and of the similar one around Melrose. This circle of defence they had learnt from Iona. Now he prayed as his fingers traced the patterns around him.

Circle me, O God,
Keep Calm within,
Keep Turmoil out.

Circle me, O God,
Keep Faith within,
Keep Doubt without.

Circle me, O God,
Keep Life within,
Keep Death without.

Before he left, Cuthbert stood up, stretched out his right arm and pointed with his finger. He turned a full circle, so that he was in the centre of it. He had made the 'Caim', the sign of the encircling God, that was so dear to the church of Iona. Now, he made the sign of the cross and said, 'Keep me, O Lord, as the apple of your eye, hide me under the shadow of your wings. Here I am, Lord, send me.'

His stay with Kenswith was amazingly brief. She saw that when God calls we must answer immediately, or too soon the vision fades. Far too often God calls and man stalls. She hastened Cuthbert on his way, sending a servant with him. There was no need for him to take anything, but Kenswith wanted him to get there with speed. So she insisted that he rode, and that the servant rode with him. She also said that he should carry his spear. It would be a shame if some petty robber would stop him now. She gave him her blessing and bade him farewell. Cuthbert could hardly travel quickly enough. Now decisions had been made, the sooner they were put into action the better. It did not occur to him that Kenswith, in sending him with horse, servant and spear, had sent him with signs of his nobility.

When he reached Melrose, nearing the monastery compound he dismounted, hugged the servant, and handed over his horse and then his spear. He said a prayer quietly as he watched the servant ride off and leave him on his own. Without any possessions, he sought entrance to the monastery.

Meanwhile, Boisil was standing at the monastery gates watching the approach of this fine young man. He felt as he watched that here was someone special. He had nothing to tell it was so, except a deep feeling. Yet he said, 'Behold the servant of the Lord.' No doubt Boisil was reflecting his reading of Saint John's Gospel, and the account of Jesus with Nathaniel. Sigfrith, who was standing near to Boisil, was most surprised at his prior's reaction. Boisil now came forward to meet Cuthbert and welcomed him, asking him the reason for his journey. There was that kind of rapport between them that is instant and rare. Here were men of differing ages, but they recognised a unity of vision and purpose. Whilst men were often kept waiting outside the monastery for days, Cuthbert was brought in and looked after by Boisil himself. In the next few days Cuthbert learnt the routine that was to become his for many years ahead, a rhythm of prayer, study and manual labour. Those few days helped him to feel more at home by the time Eata, the abbot of Melrose, arrived.

Whilst abbot and prior discussed his future, Cuthbert was left on his own. During this time, he sent up deep and heartfelt prayers to his Maker. Eata was amazed at how keen Boisil was, for he knew him to be a cautious man. Yet he bowed to Boisil's plea and agreed that Cuthbert should be admitted and receive the tonsure. Eata welcomed Cuthbert formally and invited him to join their community.

There were tears of joy in Cuthbert's eyes, as his hair was ceremonially combed and then shaved. The tonsure was in the Celtic style. They removed all the hair in the front of the head from ear to ear, allowing the hair to grow long from the middle of the head backwards. As his hair fell to the ground, Cuthbert prayed that his old life would fall away and his new road open up before him.

Now he was allowed to join the brothers. Over the weeks ahead, he approached the Rule of Life with great joy and zeal, much as he had played some of the games in his youth. He knew he was taking part in a great adventure. He was being allowed to share with the heroes of God. He was stricter on himself than the discipline asked, more diligent in times of prayer and reading, in watching before the Lord and in manual work. He often spent whole nights in prayer, sometimes even a second and third night, sleeping only on the fourth. He fasted for long periods, but was against over-long fasts in case they made him unfit for the physical work he had to do.

He learnt to live by the Rule of Columba:

> *Three labours in the day – prayers, work and reading.*
> *Take not food until you are hungry.*
> *Sleep not till you feel the desire.*
> *Speak not except on business.*

On Wednesdays and Fridays he would never eat before three in the afternoon, as was the custom of the monastery. He kept to this fasting even on long journeys.

Boisil took Cuthbert as his pupil and taught him a deep love for the Gospels, especially Saint John. The 'Eagle's Gospel' was to become his life-long study. Each day Boisil required Cuthbert to study the Scriptures and learn by heart a portion of the Psalms. It was not long before Cuthbert knew the whole Psalter, which he called 'the entire David'. Boisil, who was the expert scribe at Melrose, made sure that Cuthbert could prepare his own pens and write in a good legible script. He also taught him about work. 'Work is divided into three parts: your own work, and the work that the place you are in demands of you; secondly, a share in the common work of the brothers; lastly, helping a neighbour by instruction, or writing, or sewing a garment, or whatever the person requires.' In all this Cuthbert sought to excel with the enthusiasm of youth. It was not long before he was recognised as someone with a special fire within him and a special mission. Both Eata and Boisil marked Cuthbert out as a leader and a man with a future.

WE DWELL IN HIM

In you I live and move
And have my well-being:
God in my thinking,
God in my working,
God in my sharing,
God in my caring,
God in my deepmost soul.

In you I live and move
And have my well-being:
God in each meeting,
God in each greeting,
God in each turning,
God in each learning,
God in my deepmost soul.

In you I live and move
And have my well-being.

4

Under Orders

FOR a person who is a natural leader it is not always easy to accept the dictates of others. There were many times at Melrose when Cuthbert was tempted to lead when he was asked to follow. He had accepted authority and lived under it, though from the start his ability was recognised. Both Boisil and Eata took him into their confidence on many decision-making occasions. Cuthbert told himself he had been taught well by Kenswith, and then Boisil, about martyrdom. Now he was called to be a martyr. He was not being asked to die – that was 'red martyrdom'. But there were other martyrdoms that implied more subtle deaths. He was now being asked to leave the place and people he loved so well – that was a form of death called 'white martyrdom'. It was supposed to be the least of the martyrdoms, but Cuthbert was not so sure. His desires were also being put to the test, for he was hoping to go to Lindisfarne and they were sending him as far away from the sea as he could imagine. He had no real desire to go to Ripon. He saw the going there as a 'green martyrdom', the denial of his own desires. Still, he was being given the honour of setting up a new monastery with Eata as his leader and abbot. There would be Eata, along with twelve brothers, on the land given to them by king Alhfrith. With this, Cuthbert was not too happy. Alhfrith had shown his colours more than once, and was no lover of the Celtic church, but a supporter of Bishop Wilfrid, who favoured the Roman usage in the Church.

Cuthbert would have liked to leave Melrose by the hill route and to have gone south along the drovers' road through the Cheviots. He

could have met many of his friends on the way. They could have shared worship and communion. The hill road would have taken them to the Roman wall just as easily as Dere Street. But Eata was right, Dere Street would take them almost straight to Ripon. When they reached the wall at Corbridge, Cuthbert would have liked to follow it west to Carlisle and to the sea but that was not to be. He could only imagine himself on the high crags past Housesteads, with views back to Cheviot and across to the mountains of the west.

Setting up a monastery was something that Cuthbert did want to do. The demand for prayer and fasting was the sort of holy warfare he truly enjoyed: he relished the battle against evil. The chosen site had to be cleared not only of brushwood and stones but of its past. The place had to be cleansed of any taint of evil by prayer and fasting, before it could become a holy place, a place specially set aside for God. So the first forty days were given to prayer and fasting – almost seven weeks, for Sundays were not included. Even on Sundays the food was only a morsel of bread, a hen's egg and a little milk. This was a time of wrestling with demons and facing the powers of darkness. But the monks knew the Almighty and his power, they knew they had to be 'strong in the Lord and in the power of his might'. Moving stones and tree roots was not half as difficult as this first seven-week period: it is easier to shape a stone than a new place. At the end of their time of fasting and prayer, the brothers built the monastery and established there the same rule as at Melrose, their mother house.

Life soon settled to the pattern they were used to, of prayer, manual labour and study. From the start, there was a little group of students. There was also a constant stream of visitors, including many poor people who begged for food and shelter. All Celtic monasteries were known for their care of others. Cuthbert was made the guestmaster and was required to look after any visitors on their arrival. Whether it was the king himself or a poor man begging food, Cuthbert saw to them all. As was the custom, the unknown visitor was always treated with great care and dignity. Had not Christ said, 'As much as you did it to the least of these you did it to me'? Yet the text that more often exercised Cuthbert's mind was, 'Forget not to show your love to strangers, for thereby some have entertained angels unawares.' It made him chuckle to think of the sort of disguises angels must be turning up in if this were true. Yet he did not treat this light-heartedly. He knew well the story of Saint Martin, and understood that when Martin gave his cloak to an ordinary beggar under a bridge, he gave it to Christ. Everyone must be treated with respect and dignity as a son or daughter of God. Cuthbert was vividly aware that the one who seeks to bring Christ to another often meets Christ in that other.

One December morning before it was properly light, Cuthbert went out from the inner buildings of the monastery to the guest chamber. Here already there was a youth, white and still, though the whiteness was mainly frost and snow clinging to his clothes and making them glisten. He looked a poor creature, yet had a strange dignity, though he was obviously tired by a long journey and the snow-laden winds. Cuthbert provided him with water to wash his hands. The young man could hardly move. He watched without a murmur whilst Cuthbert removed his ragged footwear and began to rub his feet. At first touch Cuthbert felt he had been stung, and then he became used to the extra coldness. He was worried that this creature of God might die on his journey if he were not given some food. At first the youth refused, answering that he must leave quickly, for his destination was a long way off. But after many appeals, Cuthbert finally compelled him in the name of God to stay. Cuthbert then went off to morning prayers. Immediately afterwards he returned to the youth and offered him some food to eat. By now, he said, the bakehouse would be in action, and fresh loaves coming from the oven. 'Refresh yourself, brother,' he said. 'I will go and bring you a warm loaf.'

Cuthbert was not gone for long, though he did have to wait for the bread to come out of the oven. When he returned to the guest room, the young man had gone. Cuthbert hurried out to the front of the building, but there were no tracks anywhere. Fresh snow had recently fallen, and should have shown which way the man had gone. But there were no tracks at all. Cuthbert went around to the other side of the building. There was a single set of tracks which he knew were his own. Puzzled, he lifted the tray of food and went to replace it in the storehouse. As he entered, he was aware of a strangely fragrant smell. Looking about him, he saw three loaves, very white and pure looking. Was this a gift from his visitor? He had thought to feed the stranger, but ended up with food himself. The world is full of mysteries. The reading that morning had been, 'Stay awake, you never know when your Lord will come.' But Cuthbert could not get those other words out of his head: 'Do not forget to show your love to strangers, for thereby some have entertained angels unawares.' This visitation he would always remember.

Life at Ripon was far from being all dreams and visions. Much of it was hard graft. The little group were being stretched to their limits by the demands that were being made upon them. All sorts of upheavals were going on around them. Rumour had it that the kingdom itself was not all that secure. Wilfrid had returned from the continent with great pomp. He was a powerful figure and had the backing of letters from Rome. At this stage Alhfrith did not quite know what to do with Wilfrid. To keep him quiet for a while, he gave him and his followers from Rome the monastery of Ripon. Abbot Eata, along with Cuthbert and the other brothers he had brought with him, was driven out and had to head for home. The Celtic church was under threat.

The expulsion caused a great deal of sadness. There were farewells to promising pupils, and to prospective members of the community. In a short time the brothers had become attached to the place. Cuthbert, however, was quietly reciting a psalm: 'I will lift up mine eyes unto the hills, from whence cometh my help; my help cometh even from the Lord.' He was visualising the Cheviots and the Lammermuirs, and glad to be going north. He looked forward to being back at Melrose and with Boisil. Perhaps this, at last, was a move towards the island of Lindisfarne.

But there were dark clouds on the horizon. The plague was spreading again and it was no respecter of persons. Whole villages were suffering, and some small communities were being wiped out. As well as this, the Celtic mission was out of political favour. Kings and courtiers were looking to the east, to the continent and to Rome, and not to the west. It did not matter what the ordinary people felt, they would be dragged along by those in authority. Eata and Cuthbert talked long about this on their journey and afterwards. No one can live in the past. When great changes take place there is a time when the individual must also change. The people who survive are those who are able to change and yet not compromise their principles. Though they talked in theory, each knew that they were talking about the growing power of the Church of Rome. Yet they were all part of the one Church, so surely this should not be seen as a threat but an opportunity. Still, their hearts remained as heavy as the storm clouds that were gathering on the hills.

THE LORD COMES

Lord you come to us in another,
In a sister or a brother,
In a stranger or a friend,
Lord, in them you descend.
You come, Lord, in their need,
In the challenge to our greed;
You come knocking at our door
As a child or as the poor.
You come in every cry or plea,
As we respond we give to thee.
Have we met you as a friend?
You will tell us in the end.

Angels still with us share
When we show our love and care.
Holy beings fill the place
Where we show love and grace.
Let us not be unaware
Of the moment rich and rare
When the heavens do descend
Coming in a new-found friend.
Lord, let us see that you come
And seek entrance to our home.
Give us eyes and heart to see
You visit us eternally.

5

Plague Days

CUTHBERT wondered why he was so weary on his return from Ripon. Melrose did not give the joy he expected. There was another battle going on in his body. Even Boisil found it hard to raise his spirits. There was no doubt that something was wrong with him. It was soon to show itself in the colour of his skin and in the yellowing of his eyeballs. Cuthbert had caught the plague, which was now raging throughout the length and breadth of the land. The 'yellow sickness' was upon him. For most people it proved fatal; already other members of the community had died of it. Day by day Cuthbert weakened. He took to his bed and prepared himself for whatever might happen. His spirit suffered along with his body, and he felt extremely low. At this point the brothers of the monastery spent the whole night in a vigil of prayer and fasting, praying for Cuthbert's life and health. In the morning, one of the younger brothers came and told Cuthbert what they had been doing all night. Up to that point, it had been done without his knowledge. From his bed he replied, 'Why then do I lie here? For I do not doubt that God has listened to the prayers of so many good men. Give me my shoes and my staff.' Immediately he rose from his bed and with the aid of his staff began to walk. At first his steps were like the tottering of an infant, but his strength grew day by day. He made an amazing recovery, though from that time he continued to have some inner pains that did not leave him.

When Boisil saw that his dear friend had recovered it gladdened his heart. He knew that he also had caught the plague and was not far from death. 'I see, Cuthbert, that you have been saved from the

affliction that was upon you. You are a privileged person, and have been saved for a purpose. I tell you that you will not be stricken again nor are you to die soon. But now you must learn from me, as long as I am able to teach you. My own time is short, so you must lose no opportunity of learning. I know I have less than a week, if this sickness follows its course. We must use this time, as long as I can think and speak, to teach you.'

Cuthbert was deeply moved. He never doubted a word that came from Boisil, feeble as he was. To cover the great sorrow in his heart he asked, 'What is best for us to read, which we can finish in a week?'

With a keenness of eye and a new power in his voice Boisil said, 'The Evangelist Saint John. I have a book consisting of seven quires of which we can get through one every day, with the Lord's help. We can read it, and discuss it where necessary. Let us share together the Eagle's vision.'

This is what they did. They finished the readings quite quickly, for they dealt only with the simple things of the faith, and not with matters of dispute. They used the time for deep meditation rather than much conversation. These were strange days, for Boisil out of silence talked of Cuthbert's future. Cuthbert knew that Boisil was a man of great sanctity and felt each word vibrate through his whole being. Amongst other things, he suggested to Cuthbert that one day he would be made a bishop. The thought did not thrill Cuthbert – he would have preferred to be told that he would be a desert dweller for the love of God. Still, who can question the mysteries of the workings of God? He told no one of this but often talked of being a hermit, 'If only I could hide myself on a rock, where the waves of the swelling ocean surround me on every side, and hide myself from the sight and knowledge of men. Yet, I know that even there I would not be free from the deceptions of this world. Even there I would be afraid that love of wealth or honour might tempt me and lure me away.' Boisil smiled in sympathy. The last chapters of John, full of the resurrection and eternal life, were specially dear to them both. Cuthbert would remember forever the last 'Amen' as Boisil finished reading and closed the book. It was the end of the Gospel and the end of Boisil's life here on earth.

Soon after the death of Boisil, Cuthbert became the prior at Melrose. His life was now filled with spiritual direction and teaching. He became a soul friend to many. The monastery received from him wise counsel concerning life under the rule. He taught mostly by his own example and attitude. It was at this time he went out in mission to the hill country around Melrose. He ministered to people who had suffered from the plague, and he cared for the poor and the slaves. He helped to free those who had bound themselves to superstitions and idolatry. Cuthbert was always concerned about those who thought they could manipulate God through charms, amulets and incantations. He never saw prayer as manipulation, but as co-operation. Manipulation was on the side of magic, co-operation on the side of the love and power of God. He frequently visited the neighbouring villages, sometimes on horseback, but more often on foot. Here he proclaimed the power and presence of God, as Boisil had done before him.

They were good days, when people were eager to hear the Word of God. They gladly listened to what Cuthbert had to say and eagerly carried out in their actions what they could hear and understand. Cuthbert was a skilled preacher, and he loved to bring home to his hearers both the words and the Word. He looked so radiant at those times, and was so full of the Presence, that no one hid from him the secrets of their hearts. Many came to make their confession to him and to be cleansed of all their sins. Others came for healing or for the deep peace that seemed to emanate from the holy man. Wherever he went, crowds gathered in eagerness and excitement. The scenes must have been very like those by the sea of Galilee.

Cuthbert penetrated deep into the mountain areas, going where others had been afraid to go, into areas where poverty and ignorance made the people unattractive. Cuthbert saw them as children of God awaiting their redemption. Such ordinary people heard him gladly. He, in turn, attended carefully to instructing them. This meant he was often away from Melrose for two or three weeks at a time, and sometimes even a month. His own example, as well as his teaching, won over the hill people.

After such outgoing activity, Cuthbert would seek out a quiet retreat

in the hills and moors. There were many caves where he stayed, many hill tops that were familiar to him. He sought out areas where the air seemed thin and heaven close at hand. He loved border areas where earth and sky touched, or sea and land. He loved high crags that reached into the sky, meeting places of two worlds where he could encounter his Maker. It was here that he practised the discipline that gave him such control over his mind and body. But the desire that filled him most was to find a desert in the ocean. He often repeated words that were said to come from Iona, and from Columba himself:

Delightful it would be for me
To be on a pinnacle of a rock
That I might often see the
Face of the ocean,
That I might see its heaving waves
Over the wide ocean,
When they chant music to the Father
Upon the world's course.
That I might see its sparkling shore,
That I might hear the thunder
Of the sparkling waves upon the rock,
That I might hear the ocean roar
By the side of my church,
That I might see its noble flocks
Over the watery ocean,
That I might see it ebb and flow
In its career

At this point Cuthbert himself did not look to Iona and the west, but to the east coast and to Lindisfarne. That little tidal island was somehow woven into the very fabric of his life and vocation.

An Island Place

Lord, help me find
A desert place
Where I can feel
And know your grace.

Lord, help me find
A little island
Where I can feel
And know your hand.

Lord, help me find
A little cell
Where I can feel
And know you dwell.

Lord, help me find
A sacred domain
Where I can feel
And know you reign.

Lord, help me find
A special site –
Then I can feel
And know your might,

Know every place
Is full of you,
And that you fill
All, through and through.

6

Coldingham

THE whole of Northumbria began to hear of the holy man from Melrose. Monasteries and growing churches sought his attention and wanted the teaching of this man who was aflame with God. Aidan had been the torch-bearer who brought the light, but Cuthbert was now the 'fire in the north'. He knew he could not keep this fire alight without replenishing. He needed time to be on his own. The busier he became, the more he needed time to spend in prayer and in silence. Once more he longed for a little island in the sea. He loved to go to places where he could both speak and be silent. Coldingham was one such place. Perched high on the cliffs looking out over the wild North Sea was the monastery of Ebba. This was a double monastery for both men and women. It was to the north of Lindisfarne, its mother house, and on a clear day one could see the island far off, nestling in the sea. Ebba was not only the abbess, she was a princess, the sister of Oswald who had brought Aidan to Northumbria, and of the present king, Oswy. When she asked Cuthbert to come and visit he felt it was a royal command, yet he knew her humility and that she summoned him for the benefit of the monastery on the cliffs. He spent a good while there, instructing the brothers and sisters in the rule of life, opening up to them the path of righteousness, and then setting an example by deeds as much as by words. He was very fond of Ebba and enjoyed her company. He also loved to walk the cliffs and listen to the sound of the kittiwakes and see the guillemots. It was good to watch the gannets dive. Now and again he would see a dolphin out at sea, and sometimes even a whale. Great demands were being

made on him, and he took short walks between times of intensive teaching.

All this activity, rather than make Cuthbert tired, made him wide awake. Once again he was sleeping only one night in three or four. While the others were resting and sleeping he would go outside and pray. Often he would go down to the beach and let the sea water lap around him, staying there until dawn was near, and returning to the monastery for the early morning worship. During the night he would share his prayers with the curlew's cry and the seal's song. It was noticed that he often returned damp with the dew or the sea. But no one dared ask him where he had been.

One night as Cuthbert went out quietly, one of the brothers secretly followed him, curious to find out where Cuthbert went and what he was doing out there at night. The air was cool and the night was still as Cuthbert made for the shore. There, under cover of some rocks, the monk watched. For a while Cuthbert stood in cross-vigil, his arms outstretched as if on the cross. The moon was high and the monk saw a deep long shadowy cross on the sands. Even this made him nervous, for he felt he was in the presence of someone strange. For a moment Cuthbert's arms seemed to tremble, for the effort of holding them out was taking its toll. But now he waded out into the deep water, still with arms outstretched. He walked out until the swelling waves rose as far as his arms and his neck. There in the dark he sang praises, to the sound of the waves. His voice ebbed and flowed like the waters around him. A singing seal seemed to share in his song, as did the crying of a seabird and the mournful trill of the curlew. Cuthbert's prayers blended with the music of the sea. When daybreak came, as the sun peeped over the horizon, Cuthbert returned to the shore to pray yet more. Hidden in the rocks the monk remembered that the risen Jesus had stood on the shore, and he would not have been surprised if the Lord had come at that moment. Instead, out of the sea came two otters. Cuthbert, standing still, continued to pray while the otters rubbed themselves against his legs and rolled over against his feet. After a while Cuthbert lowered his hands and made the sign of the cross over the creatures. At this they moved off into the sea and swam out of sight. Cuthbert returned to the monastery in time for the early morning office, singing the canonical hymns at their appointed hour.

The watching monk was by now filled with fear. What he had seen was too overwhelming to put into words. Not only was he full of fear, but of guilt: he had been where he ought not to have been. He was sure that Cuthbert would be aware of his spying. All the way up the cliffs his heart pounded and his limbs shook. His footsteps faltered so much that he could scarcely reach home. He missed the morning office. Soon afterwards he sought out Cuthbert and prostrated himself before him. Tears rolled down his face as he asked pardon for what he had done, expecting Cuthbert to know what it was. Cuthbert could not at first understand. 'What is the matter, brother?', and as this question seemed to cause more confusion, 'What is it you have done?' Even this seemed to reduce the young man to trembling and gibberish. Slowly Cuthbert understood. 'You have been spying on me in my nightly vigil, you have been watching me whilst I have been at prayer. Now I will grant you pardon, but on this condition, that you tell no one of this before I have departed from this earth.' The promise was given and the brother was blessed by Cuthbert. He spoke to no one until after the saint's death, but then he told as many people as he could.

Not long after this Cuthbert travelled even further north. Accompanied by two of his brothers, he went by sea to the land of the Picts, to the people called the Niduari. They arrived shortly after Christmas in good weather and, expecting to make an early return, they had not brought provisions with them. But things did not turn out as they had expected. No sooner had they arrived than a great storm arose, and they were trapped for some days, cold and hungry. As the weather got fiercer their plight became worse but Cuthbert did not let the time pass without doing anything. As was his practice, he prayed day and night. On the morning of the Epiphany he spoke gently to his weary companions. 'Why do we stay here as if it were a place of safety? It will not be long before the twin enemies of hunger and cold will triumph over us. I see that the land is weighed down with snow and the sky with clouds, gales rage in the heavens and the waves of the sea are storm-swept. I know we are in great need, and there is no one near to help us. But the Lord is at hand, the Lord who opened the way through the Red Sea. The Lord is with us, who fed his children in the wilderness. He knows we are in danger. Don't let us waver in our faith. He will not allow this day to pass without food.' The brothers were amazed at the certainty of this statement, which in its own way already gave them heart. 'Look around you,' Cuthbert continued. 'He has already given us tokens of his power and his majesty. Let us bestir ourselves – I am sure he has prepared something for us.' With these words he encouraged his weary companions and led them to the shore.

There on the tide line were three pieces of dolphin flesh awaiting them, as if someone had cut the flesh and prepared it for cooking. How it came to be there they did not ask, nor did they ask Cuthbert what he did when he was away alone. He was a strange man and very strange events took place when he was present. Kneeling down, they thanked God their deliverer. Cuthbert said: 'Divine favour comes upon those who trust in the Lord. Look how he has prepared food for us. I believe each piece represents a day. We shall be here three days longer.' For the next three days the storm raged fiercely. Cuthbert's companions wondered if they were dreaming it all. Then, during the third night, the sea stopped roaring and the wind dropped. On the fourth day the promised calm arrived to bring them gently back to the south and their own land. Each man knew he had been close to death. Cuthbert's comment on this was, 'He who is afraid of death is afraid to live. It is only those who are unafraid of death that are able to venture. We shall come through many deaths, and triumph at the last, for we believe in him who gives us life that is eternal. Yet like you, brothers, I am glad that the sea is calm today.'

Coldingham

CROSS VIGIL

*The Cross of Christ
Upon this place,
The Cross of Christ
To give it grace.*

*The Cross of Christ
With arms out wide,
The Cross of Christ
That his love abide.*

*The Cross of Christ
Upon your brow,
The Cross of Christ
Protect you now.*

*The Cross of Christ
Upon your voice,
The Cross of Christ
Make you rejoice.*

*The Cross of Christ
Upon your heart,
The Cross of Christ
Set you apart.*

*The Cross of Christ
On your body whole,
The Cross of Christ
To save your soul.*

7

Food in the Wilderness

IT had been a tiring day. Cuthbert was determined to teach the young man with him by example as well as by word. Early in the morning they left the monastery for the hill country. It would be a long day of talking and walking. The lad would be expected to learn and to meditate as he went. It was a southward journey from Melrose, and then along the River Teviot. The sky was a glorious blue and promised a good day. During the journey they would recite the Psalms as they walked. Cuthbert knew them all, one hundred and fifty of them, by heart, and expected a young monk to be able to do the same in time. As they journeyed, he would recite a verse of a psalm and expect his travelling companion to respond with the next verse. By this method they would work their way through the psalter, or at least part of it. If the youth faltered, Cuthbert would recite the verse with him. Then they would go back to the beginning of that psalm, or section, and start again. Cuthbert was a peripatetic teacher, teaching as he walked. He taught a love of God's world, the understanding of nature, the use of plants, the patterns of the stars, as well as the Scriptures.

On Fridays, the journey was made harder, in that Cuthbert did not eat until the evening, and he expected his companion to do the same. Their fast was made more difficult by the hospitality of the Northumbrian people, who were always ready to share their meagre food with a traveller, and especially with a man of God. These were very poor people, who often had little food for themselves. After a very

long walk, the brothers were offered a meal in an outlying farmstead. 'We cannot eat yet, for it is a fast day,' responded Cuthbert. Instead they spent a little time in prayer and teaching about Jesus. Cuthbert used his little travelling Gospel of Saint John, taking it out of its leather satchel with great reverence. The cover was of calf skin and coloured red. He kissed it before opening it, and made the sign of the cross upon it. Today he read the account of the feeding of the five thousand. As he talked of the provision of bread in the wilderness, all the time there was a twinkle of merriment in his eyes that the youth could not help but notice. The lad also noticed that although Cuthbert opened the Gospel at the right place, he did not need to read it. He had absorbed every word of Saint John. After blessing the family, Cuthbert and his companion left for the moorland hills.

Soon they were high among the heather, though it was too early in the year for any purple. Cuthbert pressed on further and further. He was determined to get into a remote high valley. There was no human habitation now for miles, and no signs of food anywhere. It was the wrong time of the year for collecting berries or nuts. The next village on their way was small and would be very poor. Chance of a meal would be at the expense of the well-being of the residents. Yet the generosity of these folk was always humbling. At the end of a psalm, Cuthbert stopped walking and asked the youth a question. 'Where will you find food here in the wilderness? Is there someone who will offer hospitality on the way?'

The lad had long been wondering along these lines. Yet he felt Cuthbert was testing him. He had noticed that Cuthbert had brought no provisions for their journey, and he was worried that they would not complete their journey without real hardship. Strong though he was, the youth feared he might collapse on the way. All this he related to Cuthbert and confessed, 'I do not know how we will be fed here in this wild place.' All the time he noticed that Cuthbert had a glint in his eye, and that he clasped the leather satchel containing the Gospel. 'When will you learn, my son? How small your faith is! Trust in the Lord, who cares for his children in the wilderness. God will not let his loved ones perish.'

Cuthbert now began to pray quietly with his arms outstretched, making the shape of a cross with his whole body. The shadow on the ground was another cross. The boy's eyes, wide open, were on an eagle soaring overhead, encircling them and watching. Cuthbert continued to pray. The eagle suddenly dived towards the earth and from the river nearby lifted a salmon. As Cuthbert lowered his hands, the eagle dropped the salmon almost at their feet. The lad ran over and picked the fish up immediately. He loved salmon, and now looked forward to a feast. The eagle settled on the river bank to watch.

'What have you done, lad? You have robbed the fisherman of his food. This noble creature must eat also. Return to him and give him half of what there is. There is too much just for us, we cannot keep it to ourselves.'

Though a little reluctant to do it, the lad felt there was some greater justice at work than he had dreamed of. Halving the salmon with a dagger that he carried, he gently approached the bird, amazed that it did not fly off. It waited for his advances and allowed him to place the fish almost beside it. Before turning away, the lad was aware of the brightness of its eyes. Now the two moved off, the boy carrying the salmon, Cuthbert his Gospel of John. When they reached a poor dwelling, they entered and gave the fish to their hosts to be broiled. As they shared the meal, Cuthbert had the same twinkle in his eyes as before. The lad felt there was some strange alliance between Cuthbert and the eagle.

After the meal, Cuthbert drew out his Gospel book to feed the people with God's word. He explained to them that this was the fourth Gospel. Each Gospel had a symbol, and the symbol for Saint John was an eagle. It was John whose Gospel soared so high and whose vision was so bright. 'As we brought into this house a fish for refreshment, John also provides us with a fish.' At this point Cuthbert stopped and drew in the dust of the floor the shape of a fish. 'This is the sign for Jesus, the fish. In the language in which the Gospels were first written, the word for fish was ICHTHUS.' Now he drew the letters beneath the fish. 'Each letter stands for a whole word. In our language it is, Jesus Christ, God's Son, Saviour. Today, through the eagle of John, is brought to us the very Son of God, Jesus our Saviour.' Now Cuthbert kissed the book's cover. He opened it and made the sign of the cross and began to share with the people. The lad was lost in deep thought. He had learnt more than psalms today, but what he had learnt he would find hard to relate.

FOOD IN THE WILDERNESS

When our way is weary
And the going tough,

When life is dreary
And things get rough,

When spirits weaken
And the day turns dark,

When sorrows deepen
And pain finds its mark,

Strengthen us, keep us true,
Save us, Lord, as you can do.

Lord, when troubles oppress,
Feed us in the wilderness.

8

Island Days

AT last a dream had come true. After many years at Melrose, Abbot Eata transferred Cuthbert to the island of Lindisfarne. His dream upon the moors when he was sixteen had led to this. He was now following in the steps of Aidan. Soon he was doing this quite literally, for he was walking over the tidal stretch from Bee Hill shore to Lindisfarne. The tide had only recently receded. He still had to wade through the Lindis to get on to the way the monks had marked by cairns of stones. It was a direct route, yet it missed the quicksands to the right. Cuthbert thought of the many quicksands that could have engulfed the Church in the last few months. The Synod of Whitby might have been a disaster with its decision to abandon Celtic for Roman usages. Yet the Church must not be divided. It had been strange to watch the monks at Melrose, including himself, allow the hair on the front of their heads to grow, in the Roman style. For the last thirteen years he had shaved regularly, from ear to ear, all the hair on the front part of his head. Yet now it was growing well. Perhaps it would be the same with the Church, if people would only give it a chance. It was sad that Colman had left for Iona after the Synod, though Cuthbert felt a twinge of admiration, if not sympathy, for him. More sadly, as far as Cuthbert was concerned, Colman had taken with him the relics of holy Aidan. Strange, he thought as he crossed the sands, how the plague had followed the members of the Synod back to their monasteries. Did they all catch it at the Synod? He did not even want to share the thoughts of the common people who said it was a punishment from God for betraying the Church from the west. Yet his

heart was heavy as he crossed the sands. As the tide would erase his footprints, the tide of the Church from the continent was erasing the traditions from Ireland and Iona. Strange how joy and sadness run so close together. He looked up at the island that was shaped like an axe and prayed to God that he would be a faithful soldier there. He could have ridden, since he was coming as prior. But he wanted to show that he was also coming in the steps of Aidan, who had walked whenever he could. So Cuthbert walked across the sands, even though other things were being delivered for him by horse. This walking gave him time for prayer and reflection.

The welcome he was given by the brethren embarrassed him. They were so sure it was right for him to come to Lindisfarne. They had heard of his vision at the death of Aidan, and felt the time had come for Cuthbert to do the work of prior at least. Strangely enough, now that his dream was becoming an actuality, Cuthbert himself was not so sure. In his natural humility, he wondered if he would be equal to the work required of him. The island was becoming a very busy place, with its school and its many visitors. Cuthbert wondered if that was the sort of life he wanted. He was capable of organising things, but he did not see himself primarily as an organiser. Above all, he wanted to be totally dedicated to God, and to be a man of prayer.

It was good when the tide came in and the island became truly itself. There was something deep to learn from the rhythm of the tides. There is a time when contact and activity is right and necessary, but there is also a time for stillness and silence. We need to be in the throng of things, but we all need our own island of peace and renewal.

This was a time of transition for the Church, and life was not easy within the community on Lindisfarne. There were dangers of continued divisions and factions over the Celtic and Roman usages. Cuthbert had to be a great diplomat and steer a very careful path. The rule of life that he introduced at this stage was a mixture of the best of both worlds, the Celtic and the Benedictine. If arguments among the monks over the old and new ways became too heated, Cuthbert would calmly arise from his chair and leave the room, thus dissolving the chapter. He would return the next day as though the wrangling had never happened, and the brethren would be given a chance to sort out their differences peaceably. If they again resorted to heated argument, again Cuthbert would dissolve the meeting. This would continue until a more peaceful settlement was found. Amid frequent and great difficulties, Cuthbert remained calm and cheerful. His humour was something that often helped to win the day.

For all the business of the island, Cuthbert made frequent visits to the people of the area. He became known not only as a man of peace and prayer but as a healer. He grappled with demons and cured all kinds of disease. Often he was found laying hands on the sick.

Wherever he went there was a buzz of excitement over the visit of this holy man and miracle-worker. Whilst on the island he spent much time in prayer for the healing of individuals. Often, after a time of prayer, he would announce that such and such a person had been finally cured.

Throughout this time Cuthbert continued his night vigils. Often he would seek out a private spot on the north side of the island. At other times he chose the little island of Hobthrush. He preferred this island just as the tide was coming in so that he could remain there all night without being disturbed, for it was cut off for about six hours each tide. Often, as he sang his psalms, he worked with his hands to keep himself awake. At other times he walked around the island and let his psalms sing in tune with the wind and the waves. Never in this time did he seem to need much sleep. His preference was to keep awake as much as possible. He used to say, 'No one ever annoys me by awakening me from sleep. In fact, anyone who wakes me makes me glad, for by arousing me out of the heaviness of sleep, he is making me do something useful.'

Yet even Cuthbert had to admit that life was becoming too busy for him. He was not giving enough attention to his Lord and Master. He wanted more time to be alone with God. The little island of Hobthrush was too near the monastery, and he was forever being disturbed by visitors. He longed for a desert in the sea, an island where he could be alone with his Lord. At last he obtained permission from Eata and the brothers to leave and go to the Inner Farne. This island was some miles away to the south-east and surrounded on all sides by surging seas.

In the spirit of the desert monks of the early Christian centuries, Cuthbert went to Farne as a soldier of Christ to do battle with the powers of darkness. The first forty days were of particular importance, and would set much of the pattern for the future. The ground had to be prepared properly if goodness was to survive and grow there. Here Cuthbert listened at night to the singing of the seals, the startled comments of the eider duck and the roar of the mighty deep. But it was the whispers and the dark movements which he had to battle against. It was only when the soldier of Christ had conquered these, that he began to build a place fit for his rule.

He made his house as round as possible, collecting his own stones from all over the island, with the help of the brothers. One of the stones that he wanted was a good distance from the dwelling, and was so heavy it proved too difficult for four men to lift. The next day when they returned to try again, the stone was already in its place in the wall. When asked how he had managed to move it, Cuthbert would only smile, and with a glint in his eyes point heavenwards.

The great need was to have enough fresh water on the island. At the beginning Cuthbert survived by collecting rain-water in a leather sheet. So he invited some of the brothers to help him dig a pit for water. He told them that they would find the water in the very middle of his little dwelling. How he knew, they were not sure. They dug as instructed, but the place was dry. The next morning it was full of water. Though not deep, this well did not run dry, nor did it overflow and soak his dwelling.

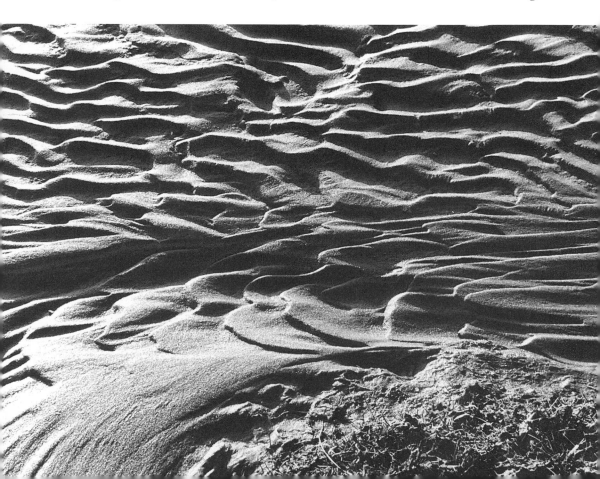

Now that his little beehive-shaped cell was complete, Cuthbert blessed it and its well. He made himself a corner for prayer and for the celebration of the Holy Communion. He knew that God did not mind the lack of trappings, for this was the God who descended to the stable. Life here would be simple but rigorous. Here the veil between heaven and earth would be drawn aside. Here he would seek to know the God who is ever present and in our midst. Here he was happy to lay aside all things to be close to his Maker.

DEDICATION

I give myself to you, Lord,
I give myself to you.

Today and tomorrow,
In joy and in sorrow,

In sickness and health,
In poverty and wealth,

In action and in rest,
I seek to give my best,

Above all to do your will,
I seek to serve you still.

Show me what I should do,
Lord, keep me true to you.

Guide me in my calling,
Let me not be stalling,

Keep me true to you, Lord,
Keep me true to you.

9

Tell it to the Birds

AT first Cuthbert could not be independent on Farne, and needed regular supplies from the brothers on Lindisfarne. Farne had never produced crops and the soil was very shallow. But following the pattern of the desert fathers, he wanted to live by the labours of his own hands. So he asked for tools and for seeds. He would be his own oxen and plough the land. He would plant seeds and so express trust in the future. However, the wheat that he had sown in the first springtime had not even begun to fruit by mid-summer. Whether it was the fault of the salt atmosphere or of the season Cuthbert was not sure. He decided that it was not the right place for wheat and asked for barley instead. 'If the barley fails to grow, I cannot become self-contained here. If I am to continue to be dependent on others, it is a sign that I should leave here and return to the monastery.' Cuthbert was making his own act of faith, for it was now long after the time for sowing barley, and he knew it. There did not seem any hope of a proper harvest. Yet when it was sown, it sprang up and produced an abundant crop. How like the Gospel, thought Cuthbert; if the right seed is sown even in a difficult climate, it will bear fruit.

Perhaps thinking of the parable of the sower had tempted Providence. For, when the crop began to ripen, some birds came and began eagerly to eat away at it. At first Cuthbert was patient, but his whole future depended on his labours bearing fruit. He could not let these creatures ruin all his plans. 'Why do you eat that for which you did not labour? Is your need greater than mine? I will not survive here without this

crop. Surely your area is larger than my small field. If you have been given permission by God, then stay, but if not, be off with you!' As he told this tale there was a twinkle in Cuthbert's eyes. 'I waved my hands as I shouted, "Be off", and the birds rose in a black cloud and flew off towards the Cheviots. They have never been seen by me since.'

Now that the invading rooks had left, the island was full of sea birds. There was also a pair of ravens who had long been in residence. In the spring, as they were nest-building, Cuthbert saw them pull at the thatch on his little guest house. They were carrying the straw away to their nest. He tried waving them off, but they ignored his gestures. So he said, 'In the name of Jesus Christ, depart and do not stay any longer in this place that you are damaging.' Scarcely had he shouted out these words when they flew away. Cuthbert watched their flight with sadness. Perhaps he had been too hasty – they would not have used much straw. He felt there was sadness in their flight that echoed in his being. He was becoming too possessive of goods, even in this small place, and wished he could make reparation. Three days later when he was digging, one raven returned. Its wings drooped and it cried in a strange croaking way. Cuthbert thought it was seeking to be friends and wanting to return to the island. That day he was gentle with it; his every gesture showed that he was willing to share what he had with this bird and its companion. Suddenly it flew off and Cuthbert felt sorry that it had gone. A couple of hours later, it returned with its mate. The flight of the second was slow and difficult, for it was carrying a large portion of pig's lard. Whenever he related the story, Cuthbert would bring out the lard and offer to grease the brothers' shoes for them. He would also take his visitors to see the nesting ravens and ask them not to disturb them.

Amongst the birds that became Cuthbert's favourites were the eider duck. The females in particular were so friendly that he often had one as his companion. In the nesting time one could be found in his little house and yet another in the guest house. Cuthbert used to love to stroke these gentle creatures each morning before his daily office. Often when he walked out he would be followed by a little group of ducklings that had adopted him as their parent. He got into the habit of sharing his thoughts with these birds. Visitors began to refer to them as 'Cuthbert's ducks'. The younger members of the community, with no disrespect, called them 'Cuddy's ducks'. Cuthbert used to say, 'We lose our relationship with creation because we have lost sight of the creator. If only we loved the creator we would learn to love his creation.' Then he would ask, 'How can you say you love the creator if you do not enjoy his creation? I fear those who can divide their religion from the rest of their work or lives.' Sometimes he would point out to sea and say, 'If you cannot understand that deep, how can you understand the great deep that you say is God?'

Cuthbert was a natural story-teller, and the brothers never knew when he was pulling their leg, yet in his humour there was always a lesson to be learned. He was forever saying that if a person fully serves the creator of all things, it is no wonder that creation will strive to work

with him. 'The very sea was ready to help me when I was in need.' The few brothers present saw the glint in his eye and knew they were going to get a story. 'I wanted a place to relieve my bodily needs, a little hut away from my dwelling. I chose a rocky site that was by the sea so that it could be washed clean twice each day with tides. But to make this possible I needed a plank at least twelve foot long, and of course not too narrow. I asked Lindisfarne for such a plank, and I was promised one but it did not come. The brothers who were to bring it returned and said they had totally forgotten about it. You can be too heavenly-minded, you know. I asked the forgetful brothers to stay until the morning, convinced that God would provide what they had failed to do. The next morning', there was a gleam in Cuthbert's eyes as he spoke, 'I took the brothers out and pointed to the sea gully I had mentioned. There across the gap was a plank exactly right. "Look what the sea has provided in the night. When people fail to heed the word of God, the wind and waves still obey him."'

MAKER OF ALL

You are the Maker
Of earth and sky,
You are the Maker
Of birds that fly,
You are the Maker
Of the oceans deep,
You are the Maker
Of moorland sheep,
You are the Maker
Of stars up above,
You are the Maker,
The giver of love,
You are the Maker
Of such as me –
Keep us all, O Lord,
Eternally.

10

Soul Friend

IT was not long before life on the little island Inner Farne was busy with people. Not only did they come from Lindisfarne and Bamburgh, but from all parts of Britain. People were attracted by the report of Cuthbert's ability to heal, and his wisdom in counselling. Many found him a soul friend with whom they could talk over their innermost secrets. Here on this sea-swept island he dealt with all the common troubles of mankind, and with some that were not so common. People openly made their confessions and others talked of their battles with temptations. All hoped to get some guidance and help from such a holy man. Nor were they disappointed in their expectations, for no one left him without feeling some form of relief from their sorrows or guilt. Cuthbert was known to be an uplifter of the downcast, a comforter of the weary, and a strengthener of the weak. At all times he reminded them that power comes from God. He never ceased to put before them the balance of things temporal and things eternal. For him there was no doubt that God was in ultimate control, and that all things would work for good. Yet he did not belittle evil. He was forever telling his visitors of the wiles of the enemy who sought to trap them. However, it is God who is almighty and through his strength we can walk through the enemy's trap as through a spider's web.

At times like this he talked of his own battle when alone on the island. On such occasions elemental forces seemed to be let loose. 'Often they would throw me down headlong from a high rock. They have thrown stones at me as if to kill me. But though they have tried to frighten me, by one attack after another, and to drive me from my

hermitage, they have not won the victory. In no way have they been able to injure my body or my mind. Nor do I fear being here alone. In fact, when the opportunity arises, I enjoy it. I actually prefer to live alone, for I know that God will never leave me nor forsake me, and my God is a mighty warrior. As for worldly wealth, I have no desire for it at all. Too many people have become possessed by their possessions. My own life is not better than the monastic life, only different. We should admire those who have put themselves under the discipline of the abbot, who have given up their own will to the will of the community and the will of God, and who have shown their deep love for God by prayers, fasting and working under the discipline of the abbot. There are many who are far more noble than me in these disciplines. The person who influenced me greatly was Boisil. His vision of the future, his predictions for me, as well as his teaching, have greatly influenced my life – though there is still a prediction to be fulfilled which I hope will not come to pass.' At this point Cuthbert would become silent and leave for his own cell and stillness. He longed for the solitary life, and did not want to fulfil Boisil's prophecy that he would one day become a bishop.

About this time, at the double monastery of Whitby, Elfleda the abbess was seriously ill. She had been suffering for a long time and had once been near the point of death. Physicians could not cure her. Though the internal pain she once felt had left her, she was unable to stand or walk. To get anywhere in the monastery she had to crawl on all fours. One day, among all her troubles, she thought of the blessed Cuthbert away to the north on his little island. 'If only I could have something that belonged to my dearest Cuthbert. If only he would send me something, I have no doubt that I would recover from this sickness.' Not long after this a messenger came from Cuthbert with a linen girdle he had recently been wearing, with his blessing. Elfleda wondered how Cuthbert had known of her wish. It is strange how sometimes messages seem to vibrate in the air. She was overjoyed at the gift, and that evening wrapped it around her habit. The very next morning she was able to stand upright and walk, with caution, and within three days she was entirely restored to health.

A few days later one of the sisters in the monastery was troubled with violent head pains. Her vision became impaired and she was unable to think clearly. It was thought that she would die. Elfleda came to visit her. Seeing the sister so afflicted, she brought Cuthbert's girdle and bound it around the sister's head. On the same day her pain left her and she was fully healed. Elfleda took the girdle and placed it in a box for safety. A few days later, when she looked for it again, it could not be found in the box or anywhere else.

On another occasion Abbess Elfleda sent a message to Cuthbert imploring him in the name of God to come and visit her to talk over matters of great importance. Cuthbert knew that such a request was not a light one, so he agreed to meet her further down the coast on Coquet Island. On this island also there was a monastery. The brothers were delighted to receive the holy man Cuthbert and the abbess Elfleda. It was a very special time for them.

For a while the two of them talked about the affairs of the monastery at Whitby. Then, suddenly, Elfleda fell at Cuthbert's feet and in the name of God with all the company of heaven she implored him to tell her how long her brother King Egfrith had to live and rule over the English people. 'I know that you have the gift of prophecy, and can tell me this if you wish.'

Cuthbert was sorry that she had invoked the name of God, for he did not truly want to speak to her of what she had asked. 'It is amazing that you, a wise woman and learned in the Scriptures, should talk in terms of the human life as if it were long. The Psalmist says that our years are reckoned like a spider's web. Solomon warns, "If a man live many years and rejoices in them all, let him still remember the days of darkness, for they shall be many; when they come the past will be reckoned as nothing." How much more, then, does he who has one year left, seem to have lived so short a time?'

At these words Elfleda wept openly. Then once again, speaking as befitted a member of the royal household, she commanded Cuthbert in the name of God and his heavenly hosts to tell of her brother's successor. Her brother had no sons or brothers. Cuthbert did not like this sort of searching and was not eager to reply. However, after a short time he said, 'Do not be afraid, he will not be without a successor. The person chosen, you will embrace with as much affection as if it were Egfrith himself.' Elfleda persisted and asked, 'I beg you, tell me where such a person is.' Cuthbert still did not wish to answer directly. He said, 'See how great and wide this sea is, and how many islands it holds? It is easy for God to choose from any of these a man to place on the throne of Egfrith.' At this point Cuthbert became silent.

Elfleda believed in her heart that he was talking of Aldfrith, who was said to be a son of Egfrith's father. At this point of time he was in Ireland studying. Elfleda did not dare pursue the matter any further. However, there was one more thing dear to her heart about which she wanted to question the holy man. She knew that Egfrith wanted to appoint Cuthbert as bishop, and she wanted to know if this was going

to happen. It would not be good for the kingdom if the holy man refused the king's request. How would Cuthbert respond? This she must approach with caution. She began in this way: 'How the hearts of men differ! Some rejoice in the riches they have gained, others who would like riches lack them. You, dear Cuthbert, despise the glory of the world, although it is offered to you. But what I would like to know is, what would happen if you were offered a bishopric? Would you be willing to leave your island, your own desert, in the service of men?'

Cuthbert was used to Elfleda's directness, but this question took his breath away. What had been prophesied seemed to be coming too close. For a brief moment he had a vision of Boisil standing there and smiling to himself. Cuthbert replied, 'I know that I am not worthy of such a position. Nevertheless I cannot escape my vocation. If God is determined to subject me to so great a burden, I believe that in a short time he will set me free. I am sure he will let me return to my island solitude. He will ask no more than two years from me. Now I command you in the name of the Lord Jesus not to tell anyone before my death of these words that have passed between us.'

Not long after this he set off northwards with the brothers for his island home. On the return journey he stopped amid the sand dunes of the port of Twyford to visit the little chapel of the dunes, overlooking Coquet Island and the sea. There he prayed for all of them – for Egfrith and Elfleda and for his own future.

We Dwell in Him

Dear Lord our God,
Help us to see Christ
In others,
Help us to receive Christ
From others,
Help us to share Christ
With others,
Help us to be Christ
To others,
Help us to bring Christ
To others.
Help us to see that
In him we live and move
And have our being,
That we dwell in him,
And he dwells in us.

11

Obeying the Vision

IT was not long after Cuthbert's visit to Twyford on the river Aln, that one of the most important events in its whole history took place. King Egfrith came with all his royal retinue, Archbishop Theodore of Canterbury came with many clergy to preside over an important Synod. The main purpose of the visit and the reason for bringing the Synod to the area was to elect Cuthbert as bishop in the Church. Theodore's idea was to split this great northern diocese and so reduce its power, though this was not on the written agenda. The main thing was to see to Cuthbert's election. This did not take much time, for all were in total agreement. Immediately, messengers and a letter were sent to Cuthbert. They sailed straight from Twyford to the Farne. But Cuthbert remained in his fastness. He sent no reply, he did not come. He was wrestling with his vocation. Now that something was moving he was more doubtful than ever. More messages were sent but the holy man did not appear. Bishop Trumwine felt that he must go and persuade Cuthbert that both the king and the Church awaited him. When he voiced this, much to his surprise, King Egfrith said he would also go and call on the holy man.

Here was one of those amazing events in the history of our country. The royal boat with all its retinue of powerful men, Bishop Trumwine and many of the clergy all came to plead with Cuthbert on the little island of Farne. There they knelt with the eider ducks around them, the kittiwakes crying, and the seals watching curiously from the sea. This was a very dangerous stretch of sea, and Cuthbert was overawed at their willingness to come to him. They pleaded with him, knelt

before him and invoked the name of God. Cuthbert knew the wrestling was over, he was called to take on the burden of being a bishop. Tears began to flow, he had become attached to his desert place. He would miss the wind and the sound of the sea, and the eider ducks who came to the touch of his hand. He agreed that he would go with the men to Twyford. As he left, he watched Lindisfarne disappear over the horizon, then Farne, then the great hill of Cheviot. The journey was not far but it seemed it was to another world.

Suddenly he was in the Synod, confronted by the king and all the dignitaries. He was suddenly aware of how cold he felt. It was not just because it was the beginning of winter, and Cheviot had a covering of snow – he feared the future. Was he the sort to be a bishop? His rough clothes stood him apart from the others. He wanted to be one of the poor of God. But he could hear Boisil telling him that his day would come. Cuthbert resigned himself to the call of God. What amazed him was the warmth and confidence of the Synod. They were unanimous in their desire that he should be made bishop.

Though winter was just beginning, Cuthbert's consecration was set to take place in the following spring, and in the meantime he was allowed to return to his island home. It had been suggested that he become the Bishop of Hexham and of the great church there. The very idea of a great church bothered Cuthbert. He was also sad that it was so far from the sea. The more he tried to become free of his island home the more attached he became to it. He wanted to be a man of prayer and a hermit rather than a bishop and organiser in the Church. One day during the winter he received a messenger from his old friend Bishop Eata, asking him to come to Melrose and meet up with him. Cuthbert crossed to the hills and spent the night in a cave. The weather was crisp and the journey to Melrose a great joy. He could not help but feel that it was Boisil who was waiting for him and wanting to help him. However, the meeting with Bishop Eata gladdened Cuthbert's heart, for Eata suggested that he himself should become Bishop of Hexham and that Cuthbert become Bishop of Lindisfarne.

On his return journey one of Egfrith's bodyguards met him and begged him to come home with him and bless his house. Cuthbert gladly did this. Then the man told him about one of his servants who was ill. He took him to the man who had the look of death rather than of sickness. His hands and feet were as if dead, and his breathing was very faint. Cuthbert asked for a bowl of water which he blessed and gave to a servant saying, 'Go, and give this to the sick man to drink.' After the third drop of this water had been poured into the sick man's mouth he fell into a deep sleep, and remained sleeping from evening until next day. In the morning when he was visited by his master, he was found to be cured. The name of the servant who administered the water to the sick man was Baldhelm. He later became a priest at Lindisfarne, and it is from him that the story of this event was handed down.

Cuthbert was made Bishop at York on Easter Day. Once again he felt how different the city of York was from his island fastness, though the whole occasion filled him with awe, and with thoughts of Boisil. Now he began to do the work of a bishop in earnest. He guarded his people with constant prayer. Once again, the busier he became, the longer he would spend in prayer. Days were spent in action and whole nights in prayer. The rigours of his monastic disciplines gave him fresh energy. He still studied and did manual work each day. Wherever he could he taught people by example rather than by mere words: he delivered the poor, fed the hungry and saw to the clothing of the naked.

Cuthbert loved visiting the high hill country and the wild windswept moors. Whenever he arrived in an area people flocked to him for his prayers and the laying on of hands. In areas where there was no church, they set up little dwellings made out of branches from trees. There they would stay for a few days. It was like something out of the New Testament, with the sick being brought to him and the people hearing him gladly. At one of these high hill encampments some women came bearing on a pallet a young man who was wasted away with a long and grievous sickness. They were afraid to approach the holy man, but one came as a messenger to ask if they might bring in the young man. Cuthbert agreed immediately. His heart went out to them all in their distress. But when he saw the state of the youth he asked them to leave him there and withdraw a little way. Then

Cuthbert prayed in earnest for this young man. He made the sign of the cross and in a loud voice gave him his blessing. Within moments the sick man got up, ate some food and gave praise to God. He returned home among great rejoicings from the women who had brought him in sickness to Cuthbert.

This was a time when many had the plague, for the pestilence attacked the whole area. Some large estates and villages were decimated, some were left with a handful of people and some with none at all. Cuthbert saw that it was his task to bring consolation and the comfort of the word of God to those who were left. In one place he asked the priest, 'Do you think that there is anyone left in these parts who needs a visit or to be comforted by us?' The priest pointed to a woman standing a little way off. Recently she had lost a son, and now in her arms was another child at the point of death. She was silent, though the tears that streamed down her face and the sorrow of her whole stance told of her troubles. Immediately Cuthbert went over to her and gave her his blessing. He then kissed the boy on the head. 'Fear not, do not be distressed, for your child will be healed. No one else in your home will be taken by this plague. The love and light of the Lord be upon you.' Many years later this woman and her son would tell of this moment.

In all his caring for others Cuthbert was aware of his own sickness. Years of hard work and spending himself in the service of others were taking their toll. He decided that he no longer had the strength for journeying around his diocese. It was time for him to lay aside the office of bishop and to return to his island. Life was waning like the tide. He must now free himself from worldly demands and turn his face only to his Maker. The thought of this made him want to go around his diocese yet once more, and to visit the many hill places that were familiar to him, although by now this demanded tremendous effort.

On this last visitation, at the request of the abbess Elfleda, he came to her monastery to dedicate a church. He was glad to think of the churches he had planted and the seeds he had sown. During the feast before the dedication, Cuthbert sat quietly. Suddenly his knife fell from

his hands, his face lost all its colour, his limbs were rigid and his eyes stared wide. He had the look of a man who had seen something terrifying. A priest nearby, noticing this, bent towards Elfleda and whispered, 'Ask the Bishop what he has seen, I am sure that this spasm is not without cause. There is something affecting the holy man's life which we are unable to see.' Immediately Elfleda gave Cuthbert her attention and asked what it was that he had seen. Cuthbert came to himself at once and tried to hide the fact that anything had happened by saying, 'Can I eat all day? I need rest sometimes!' Elfleda persisted, so Cuthbert said, 'I have seen a holy man being taken up into the kingdom of heaven.' 'From where?' asked the abbess. 'From your estate', Cuthbert replied. But when she asked for his name, Cuthbert was not able to tell her. 'However, tomorrow at the mass you will tell me yourself that I may pray for him.' Elfleda enquired if there were any on the estate that had died but it seemed there was none. However, the next morning early she was told that a shepherd, a man of good life, had fallen from a tree and died immediately. This had happened at the very hour that Cuthbert had mentioned it at the table. She went to the bishop and said, 'I pray you, my lord bishop, remember at mass Hadwald my shepherd.' Cuthbert always said to the people, 'Beware of wanting to have visions for they need not be for your own good.'

YOU CAN MAKE US WHOLE

Only you, Lord,
Can make us whole,
Only you, Lord,
Can save our soul.
Keep us at dawning,
Keep us this morning,
Keep us at sunset,
Keep us in darkness.
When our way is hard,
Be you, Lord, our guard,
When the way is steep
Keep us, Lord, keep.
When we are ill,
Protect us, Lord, still.
Only you, Lord,
Can make us whole,
Only you, Lord,
Can save our soul.

12

Fire of the North

THROUGHOUT his preaching tours Cuthbert saw himself as a soldier of Christ. This was no gentle mission, it was into hostile territory. Often the country he travelled was already occupied by the old enemy. There would be opposition, there would be battles. Sometimes the conflict was subtle, unseen to anyone but himself. At other times there was open war, which was terrifying to see. Cuthbert knew that there were times when the only way to fight fire was with fire. To check the fire spreading he had to create a fire break of his own, and no one could do this who was afraid of being burnt. To be a light he had to be willing to be burnt. Cuthbert always reminded people that it is hard to live life to the full if one is afraid of death. Once in the middle of some teaching he stopped and said, 'Beloved, whenever you hear of the mysteries of the kingdom of heaven, you must be on your guard. Keep a watchful eye and an attentive ear, stay alert, or the old enemy, the devil will invade you. He has a thousand tricks and wiles to prevent you from hearing of eternal salvation. It is those who strive to do good that should expect opposition.' Almost at once, a nearby house in the village caught fire, or so it seemed. Great sparks fanned by the wind leaped from house to house, a great crackling rent the air. The whole village, who had been listening with great attention to Cuthbert, now sprang up to tackle the blaze. Cuthbert held a few of them back, and they remained behind his outstretched arms like children hiding behind a cross. Now water was being thrown onto the flames, but the crackling continued and the flames did not die away. As Cuthbert, still in cross-vigil, began to pray, his voice became louder

than the crackling. Soon the fires died down as speedily as they had arrived. The crowd returned to him full of wonder and sat again at his feet. He told them that they had been tricked: this was no real fire, but the evil one trying to capture their minds. The evil one is always ready to fill us with delusions. The people flocked to him again without any distractions, though some cast nervous glances back at the house that appeared to have burned.

There was a time when Cuthbert returned to Wrangham to visit his foster mother, Kenswith. Whenever he could he visited her, for he owed her a great deal. It was Kenswith who had taught him much that he knew, and had schooled him in many of the mysteries. Her house was at the west end of the small village. Cuthbert had not long been with her when a house at the eastern side of the village caught fire through someone's carelessness. There was a mighty wind blowing which fanned the flames. Blazing thatch was spreading from the roof of one house to another. Soon the whole village was in danger of being alight. Every able hand was at work carrying water, but the fierceness of the flames drove them back. Kenswith, who had gone out to visit a neighbour, came in breathless and agitated. She pleaded with Cuthbert to help before the whole village was ablaze. 'Don't be afraid, mother. You must not panic. This fire will not harm you or any of your friends.' Cuthbert then went outside into the wind and the smoke. Flames filled the evening sky with redness. But even now Cuthbert felt that a change was on its way. He prostrated himself upon the ground. His prayers were strange and rhythmic, more in tune with the wind than with words. At once the direction of the wind changed and so the village was saved, apart from the house where the fire started. People knew that Cuthbert had lain on the ground and that about that very moment the wind had changed. The story of this was to stay in the village for a very long time.

Kenswith knew better than to ask questions. All that Cuthbert would say is, 'God's power is always mightier than men's efforts. When we pray strange powers are set at work, and when we do not pray we hinder those powers. There are times when we must fight fire with fire. In these dark days we are called to be the fire in the north.'

In his travels, Cuthbert often called on a sheriff of King Egfrith called Hildmer. He and his wife were given to good works and to furthering the gospel. They were a good example to all they served and all who came in contact with them. However, Hildmer's wife was often attacked by a demon that afflicted her sorely. She rolled her eyes and gnashed her teeth, crying piteously. Her limbs flailed until she dropped. All who saw this were terrified. When she fell it was as though she were dead – in fact some said she was dead. Once she had a severe attack and did not regain conciousness. Her husband knew the man of God was in the district, so he got on his horse and came to him. He pleaded, 'My wife is ill and at the point of death, I beg that you will send a priest before she dies. She longs to receive the blessed sacrament, and I beg that you will permit her to be buried in holy ground.' Cuthbert was about to send a priest, when he realised the oddness of the request. Why should she not be buried in holy ground? Why had Hilmer not asked Cuthbert himself to come? There was something that his friend had hidden from him. Turning to him he said, 'I must not send anyone else, I will come to her myself.' As they returned the sheriff began to weep and pour out the troubles of his heart. Inwardly he was afraid that Cuthbert would say that her sickness was through sin or a lack of faith. Cuthbert again sensed his friend's fears. 'Do not be afraid, as though I might find your wife in a state that I am not aware of. I know, though you will not admit it, that she is afflicted with a demon. I also know that before we arrive the demon will have left her. She will come to meet us joyfully as if it had never been. She will take the reins of the horse and bid us enter the house as usual. You must know, my friend, that the evil one attacks the best of people. In fact it is the righteous that seem to be singled out for attack. If you are good you should expect opposition from the evil one. It is only if you are wicked that you should expect the demons not to oppose you.' Much of this was lost on Hildmer at the moment, but he did realise that Cuthbert did not equate sickness with sin.

As Cuthbert had forecast, when they arrived, the woman was already recovered. She had arisen as out of a deep sleep, as if she had thrown off shackles from her limbs. She ran forward and took the bridle

of Cuthbert's horse and urged them to come into the house. In later
years she said that from the moment she touched the bridle, a fire
burned within her and she was freed from her affliction. She testified
many years later that her illness never did return.

On another occasion sheriff Hildmer himself took seriously ill. His
breathing came in short gasps and there were very long intervals
between each breath. His friends had met to try and offer him comfort
and at least the support of their presence. One of them suddenly
remembered that he had in his pocket a piece of bread which Cuthbert

had blessed shortly beforehand. 'Cuthbert has blessed this bread and prayed for us that it would be for us the bread of life. I pray you, brother, partake of it.' Hildmer's breathing became a little more regular even at the mention of the name of Cuthbert. How he wished he were here now! As he was not present, he would make do with the bread blessed by the holy man. But he knew he would have great difficulty in swallowing anything. Through signs rather than words, Hildmer asked them to put a small piece of the bread in his drinking water. Once this was done he slowly drank from the cup. The moment he sipped the water his breathing became more regular and he began to relax. Later he said from that moment the pain left his stomach. From then on his health and strength returned and his body began to fill out again. All who heard of this said it was due to Hildmer's own faith, but also to the holiness of Cuthbert.

LIGHTEN OUR DARKNESS

Lighten our darkness,
Lord, we ask,
Lighten our darkness,
Guide our task.
Lighten our darkness,
Dispel the night,
For the love of Jesus,
The Lord of light.

Lighten our darkness,
Make our days bright,
Lighten our darkness,
Give us clear sight.
Lighten our darkness,
Until life is done,
For the love of Jesus,
Our Lord, your Son.

91

13

Visions

MORE than once in his life Cuthbert showed himself to have 'the sight', that is, he seemed to be able to see beyond the obvious, and even beyond the present moment. No doubt some of this was simply the sensitiveness of a man who always set himself to be open-eyed and open-minded. At other times it was because he understood how to read the world around him and to interpret its messages. There were yet other times when it was just a 'feeling' without absolute clearness, but an awareness that great events were taking place. On these occasions it was up to his listeners to interpret the events when they happened. Then there were still other occasions when 'the sight' defied all known explanations, but told of the mysterious link that we humans have with each other and with all things. These times witnessed to the fact that we are not separate entities, but that there are strands that keep us linked together, and these strands can be made to vibrate.

King Egfrith had taken his army into the kingdom of the Picts, and was devastating their territory with ferocity and great daring. At this time Cuthbert came to the town of Carlisle to speak to the queen, who was in her sister's monastery awaiting the outcome of the war. The people of Carlisle, proud of their past, were showing Cuthbert the city walls and a fountain dating from Roman times. Near this fountain Cuthbert was suddenly troubled in spirit. He groaned and looked to the ground, not wanting to face anyone. At last he stood erect, looked heavenwards and in a low voice whispered, 'Perhaps even now, at this very moment, the issue of the battle is decided.' A priest standing by,

knowing of whom he spoke, asked, 'How do you know?' Cuthbert did
not want to say more but pointed to the sky. 'Do you not see how
disturbed the elements are? There has been a sudden change. What
mortal man is able to inquire into the deep things of God?' Immediately
Cuthbert went to the queen himself. 'You must enter your chariot early
on Monday and go into the royal city quickly, just in case the king has

been killed. I would say go tomorrow, but it is the Lord's day and it is not proper for the queen to travel. Tomorrow I have a church to dedicate at a neighbouring monastery. Once this is done I will come to you.'

The dedication of the church went smoothly and the brothers were complimenting Cuthbert on his sermon when suddenly he said, 'Beloved, I implore you to be alert. As the Apostle Paul says, stand firm in the faith, lest some temptation may come and find you unprepared. The Lord himself said, "Watch and pray that you enter not into temptation".' His hearers thought he was prophesying a return of the plague that only recently had been devastating the area. But he continued, 'Once while I was living alone on my island, some of the brothers came to me on the feast of our Lord's Nativity. They asked me to leave my dwelling place, that I might celebrate the day joyfully with them. I did as they requested and we sat down to feast in the guest house. Suddenly in the midst of it I said to them, "I beseech you brothers, let us be careful, and watch and pray. It is possible we could be led into temptation by carelessness and recklessness." They replied, "O come, Cuthbert, let us at least be joyful on the day of our Lord's birth." "So be it", I replied. Once more they entered into feasting and story-telling and I saw danger at hand. I warned them again. This time they said, "O come on, Cuthbert, we have plenty of fast days, prayer days and vigils – let us have a bit of fun today." I again said, "So be it." But a third time I was troubled, and warned them that if they did not take care they would be in great danger. So this time they agreed with me to be alert to the wiles of the devil. I can only tell you I knew for sure that trouble was near.

'We did not know why all this took place but the next morning when they went back to Lindisfarne, they found one of their number had died of the plague. From then it grew worse day by day for almost the whole of the year. Most of the congregation of Lindisfarne died at this time and there was great sorrow in our land.'

It was because of this account that the monks felt that he was talking of the plague returning to them. But the very next day someone returned from the battle and his story explained the foreboding of the

man of God. At the very day and hour that Cuthbert leaned on his staff by the fountain, the king fell by the sword and his bodyguard was killed defending him.

Soon after this Cuthbert returned to Carlisle to ordain some as priests, and to clothe the queen herself in the monastic habit. Whilst he was there he was visited by a dear friend, Herbert. For a long time the two had been soul friends, Cuthbert on Farne and Herbert on a little island in the Derwent lake. For a good many years Herbert had travelled each year to Cuthbert for teaching and spiritual matters. He had heard that Cuthbert was staying in the city and made a point of coming to see him. At the end of their time together, Cuthbert said, 'Remember, Herbert, to ask me now for whatever you need. Speak to me about it now, for once we part, we shall never see one another again on this earth. I am certain that the time of my departure from this world is at hand. I have not much longer to live and that I know.'

When Herbert heard this he fell at Cuthbert's feet in tears, and with great sorrow asked, 'I beseech you by the Lord not to leave me. Ask the merciful God, as we have served him together on earth, that we may journey together to his kingdom in the heavens.' Cuthbert was deeply stirred by this sign of affection. For a good while he did not move, but stood in silent prayer.

Then suddenly he spoke. 'Rise, dear friend and brother, do not weep but rejoice. Our God has given us what you have asked.' No more was said by either of these saintly men. Herbert suffered from a long and painful illness. On the day that Cuthbert died Herbert entered into a deep and peaceful sleep. It could be seen from his face that all pain and suffering had now left him, and later on the same morning he entered into the fullness of eternal life. While Cuthbert was being buried in the church of Lindisfarne, Herbert was also buried on the little island in the lake Derwent which had been his hermitage. There is no telling what it is that links lives and minds but whatever it is, it is deeper than our understanding.

Cuthbert knew that his old illness had returned, and that he was becoming less able to fulfil the arduous duties of a bishop. Now he made his decision and set his face to the east and to his beloved Farne.

This time as he travelled along the Roman Wall he did so with deep feeling for he would not travel this way again. Up on the high crags near the Roman fortress of Housesteads he looked at the loughs reflecting sunlight. 'Pools of light, pools of light, Lord, may we ever be pools of light and a fire in the dark.' He looked beyond the Wall to far off Cheviot, then to the right of it. Somewhere there hidden from sight was his earthly home and the place of preparation for his last great battle.

To See Beyond

Open our eyes
To see beyond the familiar.
Extend our vision
To behold the mysteries.
Make us aware
Of your Presence and power.
Increase our sense
Of ability and purpose.
Make us heed
Your word and call.
Help us be sensitive
To your coming in others.
May we reach out
And know we touch you.

14

Last Days on the Farne

SO having spent two arduous years travelling his diocese and caring for the poor and the sick, Cuthbert gave up his position as bishop. He knew that he did not have long left on this earth and he wanted to use the time left to prepare himself to meet his Maker. He returned to the Farne Island, that was like a balm in itself, with its sea-light mornings and evenings, and the pools of light among the rocks. He felt he was back home.

One day, some of the brothers came for instruction and words of encouragement. After it was ended Cuthbert said, 'I must now return to solitude, but before you leave take some food. That goose hanging on the wall – cook it and eat it. Then you can board your vessel and return home.' Cuthbert then entered his dwelling. The others ate the food that they had brought, but left the goose as they had plenty of provisions. After the meal they were about to board the vessel when a fierce storm arose and prevented them from sailing. For several days they were shut in by raging seas. All this time the goose hung on the wall. When they went to Cuthbert to complain about the delay of their return, he asked them to be patient. It was on the seventh day that Cuthbert arrived at their dwelling house and warned them about the sins of disobedience. He had that old twinkle in his eye when he said, 'Doesn't the goose still hang there uneaten? You have not done what I asked of you. No wonder the sea is against you. Quickly, put it in the pot and cook it, eat it and then the sea will be quiet again.' They

did as they were told. As soon as the goose began to boil in the pot the wind ceased and the waves lessened. By the time the meal was finished, they were able to board their boat on a calm sea. Cuthbert smiled to himself. These poor illiterate monks, they could read books but not the weather. They knew their alphabet, but could not read the earth or sky. One day they might become more sensitive.

Cuthbert went to Lindisfarne for the feast of the Nativity at the request of the brothers. As he prepared to return to the Farne a great crowd of them came to see him off. An aged monk made weak by dysentery but still strong in the faith asked, 'Tell us, Lord Bishop, when we may hope for your return?' It was a straight question and it got a straight reply: 'When you bring my body back here'. This caused a murmur of alarm. But Cuthbert would not let them make anything of it. He insisted that he be allowed at that moment to set out for home.

He was to have more than two months on the island that he counted as home. He rejoiced in the quiet, he welcomed sunrise and sunset, he delighted in the light on the water. Here his old disciplines of mind and body really came into play. His illness began on a Wednesday and continued for three weeks. On the first day Herefrith, who was on the island with some of the brothers, gave Cuthbert a signal that he was approaching his dwelling. Cuthbert only answered the greeting with a moan and told of how he had been attacked with illness during the night. As they were used to Cuthbert being ill these days, Herefrith asked a blessing before they left. 'Do as you say, get aboard your vessel and return home. Then, when God has taken my spirit, bury me in this dwelling near my oratory towards the south, on the eastern side of the cross I have erected there. I have hidden a sarcophagus, which the abbot Cudda once gave me, under the turf on the north side of the oratory. Place my body in this and wrap it with the cloth you will find there. I was unwilling to wear this cloth whilst alive but out of love for the abbess Verca, I have taken care of it for this very purpose.'

Heretrith was startled by all this talk of death and said, 'I beseech you, father, let some of us stay here and minister to you.' Cuthbert quietly and firmly refused saying 'No. Go now, and when God wills that you should come again he will direct you.' Herefrith tried in vain to be allowed to leave one of the brothers, though it was obvious that Cuthbert wanted to be left alone. As soon as Herefrith and the monks returned he called all of the brothers to the church and commanded that prayer should be made without ceasing for Cuthbert. 'For it seems almost certain that the time of his departure is at hand.'

Herefrith was keen to return to the Farne and see to the ailing Cuthbert but for five days a storm prevented them. The sea rose in mountainous waves and its roar could be heard all over the island. When the storm ceased they set off in their boat. On landing they found Cuthbert not in his own dwelling but in the guest house that he had built. The brothers had to return to Lindisfarne, but Herefrith remained. He bathed Cuthbert's foot which was swollen; it had a suppurating ulcer that needed treatment. The poor man was now weary by lack of food and by disease. Herefrith managed to persuade him to take a little heated wine. All the time Cuthbert was silent. Herefrith said, 'I see, my lord Bishop, that you have been severely ill since we left. You should have let one of us stay.' In a faint voice Cuthbert replied: 'As soon as you left, my illness became worse. I came to this place so that when you arrived you would find me here and not need to enter my dwelling. I have been in this place five days and nights without moving.'

'But how could you survive this time without food?' In answer, Cuthbert drew back the coverlet of the bed on which he was sitting and revealed five onions. 'This has been my food whenever I was hungry.' Herefrith noticed that only one onion showed any signs of being nibbled at. 'But this has been a time of great battle against the old enemy. I have fought the fight and finished the course.' With these last words a great vigour returned to his voice.

Herefrith then persuaded Cuthbert that he did now need someone to look after him and from that day they did. Herefrith returned to Lindisfarne and told how Cuthbert wanted to be buried on his own island. 'But I think it is more fitting that we persuade him to allow us to bring his body here and bury it with due honours in the church.' Of this all the brothers were sure, that Cuthbert should come to Lindisfarne. Herefrith made a cautious approach to Cuthbert on his next visit. 'We did not dare, my lord Bishop, to disobey your command to bury you here, but we ask that you count us worthy of the honour of your presence in death. We would like you to be buried on Lindisfarne as befits a bishop.'

Cuthbert looked with sad eyes. 'It was my desire that my body should rest here where I have fought my fight for the Lord and from where I hope to rise to be with him in glory. It would be more expedient for you if I were to remain here. I see that fugitives and guilty men will seek sanctuary where I lie. You will have difficulties with the powers of this world if you allow this to happen. The presence of my body may cause you much disturbance.' For all his talk Cuthbert saw that his request still grieved the brothers, so he continued, 'If you wish to take me away from here, it would be better if you bury me in the interior of the church. Then you will have some control over who can come in or not.' At this the brothers were delighted, but they failed to see the great sorrow in the old man's eyes.

Cuthbert commanded that he be taken back to his little oratory. Because of his weakness he was carried there by four of the brothers.

Though no one had been allowed to enter his dwelling, Cuthbert was persuaded to let one monk enter and stay with him. Cuthbert looked about and chose Walhstod. 'Let Walhstod enter with me.' For a long time this brother had also been ill but when he left Cuthbert six hours later he declared himself to be cured and well. Time proved this to be true. Cuthbert however declared that if he had any power in these matters, surely he would have cured himself.

Soon after this Walhstod, entering the oratory again, found Cuthbert lying in the corner opposite to the altar. His end was now near and he found great difficulty in speech. He talked of humility and peace and how we need be on our guard against those that fight against them. He said, 'Always keep peace and godly love among yourselves. When necessity forces you to see about your affairs see to it that you are not divided in your counsels. Always live in mutual agreement with the other servants of Christ. Do not cease to be hospitable to all who come. Do not think that you are better than others in the same faith and manner of life. Have no communion with those who depart from the unity of the Catholic peace of the Church. And you are to know that if necessity compels you to choose one of two evils, I would much rather you took my bones from the tomb, carried them with you and departing from this place dwelt wherever God ordained.'

The day passed; every now and again Cuthbert spoke quietly, and through the evening he continued praying and saying the psalms. At the accustomed time of evening prayer he received his communion for the last time on earth. After this he lifted his hand high in praise and departed to his Father.

TIDE CHANGE

The tide ebbs –
Darkness will come –
Draw me, Lord,
To your home.
The waves are high –
The storms increase –
Draw me, Lord,
To your peace.

The tide will turn –
The tide will flow –
I to the Lord
My God will go.
The storm will ease –
The wind will cease
The Lord will come
And bring release

The ebb and the flow,
As it was
It is and shall be
For ever and ever,
And ever more.
The flow and the ebb,
As it was
It is and shall be,
Until I reach
The eternal shore.

15

Death and Beyond

WALHSTOD rushed out from the little hut to tell the brothers who had spent the night in prayer and vigil. At that moment they were singing Psalm 60: 'Oh God, you have cast us off and broken us: you were enraged against us, O restore us again. . . . O save us by your right hand and answer us: that those whom you love may be delivered.'

Immediately, one of the monks went out and lit two torches; holding one in each hand he went to the higher ground to the north-west of the island and gave the agreed signal to Lindisfarne that the holy man had gone to his eternal home. At Lindisfarne a brother had been peering into the night waiting and watching. He was now weary and cold, and would rather have been at prayers with the others. At first he thought that his eyes were deceiving him, but then he saw for sure glimmers of light from the torches. The 'light of the north' had gone out. From overhead came the sound of a flight of geese. The monk signed the direction of the Farne with a cross and then signed himself. He then left his watch tower and ran to the church where the brethren were gathered together for the same office of Lauds. When he arrived they were actually singing the same words of the psalm, 'O God you have cast us off and broken us'.

They continued the psalm though they knew why the brother had entered the church. The words seemed full of threats and foreboding. As events unfolded in the months to come, it was as if the psalm was being fulfilled. After Cuthbert was buried a great storm arose on the island, the winds blew and for a while winter returned. The fire had

gone out. The brothers themselves became storm-tossed in the months ahead. Many left the island never to return. Others talked of the strange elements that had reasserted themselves as soon as the holy man had died. It was as if he had been holding back many dark forces and now they were determined to get loose.

There was a whole year of troubles and only when Eadbert was ordained as bishop were the storms and disturbances driven away. Only then did the latter part of the psalm find its fulfilment: 'By the power of God we will do valiantly: for it is he that shall tread down our enemies.'

A boat was sent to Farne to bring back Cuthbert for his burial. It was a calm day on the south shore of the island where they landed. They could see Cheviot snow-capped, and Lindisfarne lying on a calm and slightly misty sea. The seals came out to watch and the eider ducks were holding animated conversations. The kittiwakes were also heard crying. The sea was strangely calm for their voyage.

At Lindisfarne they were met by a great company of people, choirs and singers. The church was full and people were standing outside. As the boat landed the choir began to sing and commend their beloved to the fullness of life eternal. In the church of St Peter the fisherman, a grave had already been prepared at the right hand of the altar and the stone sarcophagus awaited him. This hole in the ground seemed to many like the hole that was in their hearts. Cuthbert was wrapped in the fair linen cloth dipped in wax given to him by the abbess Verca, and dressed in priestly vestments, with shoes on his feet. An unconsecrated host was placed on his breast. His soul was commended to his Maker, whom he knew so well, to his Saviour whom he served so faithfully, and to the Spirit who had filled him from the beginning. The holy man had completed his pilgrimage; now it was his birth day in the heavenly kingdom.

Each of the brothers in turn came and threw a handful of soil on the coffin and signed the grave with the sign of the cross. Slowly it was covered whilst the choir continued to sing and commend him to God. The earth filled the dark hole. Cuthbert was blessed. The Fire of the North shone out in the kingdom of heaven.

After his death many miracles were recorded at his tomb. People still flocked to be near the resting place of the body of the holy man. The island became more than ever a place of pilgrimage. Stranger still were the events that took place eleven years after his burial. It had been agreed at that time to dig up the remains, to wash the bones and put them in a place above ground so that they might be seen and venerated. The day chosen was the day of his burial, which is the 20th of March. On opening the sarcophagus they found the body intact as on the day of his burial. He looked as if he were still alive, more like a man relaxed in sleep than a man who had been dead for eleven years. The garments he was buried in were not soiled but looked new and strangely bright. Everyone was overcome with awe and a little afraid. They were standing before something strange, a great mystery. After a while they had the courage to remove the uppermost garment but dared not proceed any further. News was sent to Eadbert of what they had found. At the time he was in retreat not far from the church, for he was on the little island that they were beginning to call 'Cuthbert's island'. In the tradition of the saints of the island that had gone before him, Eadbert used to spend the time of Lent and Advent there, in deep devotion, fasting and prayer. It was there that Cuthbert had chosen to pray in the seasons of penitence before he went to the Farne for greater solitude.

Here on the little island they offered Eadbert the outer garment of Cuthbert. As he took it the sun shone and the west wind blew. It seemed to float in his hands. He kissed the garment with affection holding it with reverence. 'Put fresh clothes around the body, and then replace it in the chest we have prepared. As for the grave, it will not long remain empty. Blessed is the man whom the Lord will allow to rest there.' As he marvelled, he added these words:

What tongue can talk about the things of God?
What eye has seen the joys of paradise?
That is only for those that leave this world
For the ark of heaven, for the Lord himself.
See how God honours the earthly body –

What a token of things to come!
You have let our church be filled with paradise,
You have held back decay in blessed Cuthbert,
That we might know that life is eternal.
When the last trump will sound,
You will raise us to glory for your Son's sake.

When the bishop, still windswept and elated, had finished speaking, with great emotion and tears, the brothers did as he commanded. Cuthbert's body was lifted into the light casket prepared for it, clothed in new garments and with all the symbols of his holy office: his cross, a chalice and paten, a small silver altar, his staff, his stole, and his shoes, along with a comb and a small pair of shears. The coffin in which he was laid was placed above his old resting place so that all could view the saint.

Meanwhile Bishop Eadbert took ill. He did not recover his strength, but weakened day by day. In just over a month, that is on the 6th of May, he was buried in the grave of his dear friend the blessed Cuthbert. Over his tomb was placed the coffin in which lay the uncorrupt body of Cuthbert. The Lindisfarne Gospels, written 'to the glory of God and in memory of Cuthbert', were placed near the coffin.

From now on pilgrims from all over the land flocked to the tomb of one of its most holy people. Miracles, healings and answered prayers all became part of the life of the little island. As many people came to Cuthbert after his death as had done in his lifetime.

As the Venerable Bede recorded the death of Cuthbert, he wrote in his *History of the English Church and People*:

'Above all else he was afire with heavenly love.'

COME, LORD JESUS

Between me and the darkest night,
Between me and the failing light,
Between me and the loss of sight,
COME, LORD JESUS.

Between me and the fears that cower,
Between me and the waning power,
Between me and the final hour,
COME, LORD JESUS.

Between me and all that would deprave,
Between me and the deadly wave,
Between me and the earthly grave,
COME, LORD JESUS.

16

Cuthbert's Folk

THE pilgrims who flocked to Lindisfarne after Cuthbert's death brought gifts and enriched the small community that maintained life on the island. The shrine of Cuthbert with its coffin-reliquary became one of the holy places that had to be visited. The pilgrims' way was well trodden when the tide allowed. The island was looked upon as a major centre of Christianity, a place of real importance. Everyone who lived there benefited in some way, and life was both interesting and busy. Then in 793 calamity struck. The year had been a bad one with violent winds and great electrical storms, but real trouble came from the sea – Viking sea raiders appeared on the horizon. From that moment the monks were in no doubt about their danger. These men were out for spoil and they were certainly no respecters of person or of church. At the best, superstition might keep them from doing some things. The people at Bebbaburgh and all along the coast watched in dread. Slowly but surely it became obvious that the first place of attack would be Lindisfarne – the boats were making straight for the island.

A hurried meeting was held and a decision made to leave the island. There was not a moment to lose. Bishop Highbald ordered his community to collect what treasures and communion vessels they could and flee to the mainland. They would put the Kyloe hills between them and the invaders, for the hill country would be far safer than the coast. However, when it came to it, some monks decided to remain and look after the holy place. They were men of peace, so even if the raiders took the treasures they themselves should be unharmed. Highbald tried briefly to persuade them otherwise, for these raiders did

not have a reputation for kindliness. Those that stayed were risking their lives.

The raiders were out for plunder and to show their power to conquer. The island was chosen carefully as offering easy pickings and as an example. They took any silver and gold that had been left, smashed altars and broke down the high cross placed there by Bishop Ethelwald. The monks could not stand by and watch this and they put up some resistance. Several members of the community were killed, others were drowned in the sea, and yet others were taken away as slaves, when the raiders left.

When those who had gone to the mainland cautiously returned they were shocked at what they found, and this shock wave travelled all over the continent. Alcuin wrote from the court of Charlemagne to King Ethelred, 'Never before has terror appeared in Britain such as we have now suffered from a pagan race, nor was it thought that such an inroad from the sea could be made. Behold the church of Cuthbert spattered with the blood of the priests of God, despoiled of all its ornaments; a place more venerable than all in Britain is given as prey to pagan peoples.'

Yet for some strange reason the shrine of Cuthbert had escaped damage. Life at the monastery slowly returned to normal. Pilgrims were fewer, for these were dangerous times. The invasions were more sporadic on the east coast but they did continue, and eventually Bishop Ecgred decided that the island was no longer a place of safety. He made the unusual decision to move not only Cuthbert's body and the monks, but the church building also. The church was dismantled piece by piece and moved inland to Norham on the river Tweed. Here it was hoped that a new centre of pilgrimage would grow.

Then a fiercer round of invasions began. Tynemouth priory was totally destroyed. Monkwearmouth and Jarrow monasteries were plundered and ruined, the great Hexham was set alight and destroyed. This time they were aware of what was coming. Someone then related the words of Cuthbert, that if ever the monks were to leave they should take him with them on their journeying. So the wooden coffin with its elaborate carvings was put upon a cart. Other relics, including the head of King Oswald, and some bones of St Aidan were placed in a linen bag inside Cuthbert's coffin. They covered it all over with bull's hide to protect it from the elements. It was in the year 875 that they left their new-found home, on the rumour that Halfdan of the Wide Embrace was coming north with a great Viking force.

There did not seem anywhere safe for them, so they headed west, hoping to get to Ireland. On the journey they went past the Lammermuirs where Cuthbert had his vision, and on past Melrose where he was trained. From there they also came to the Derwent and near to the place where Herbert was buried. In death Cuthbert was being brought back to all the places he had served so well. However, even Cumbria was not as safe as they had hoped, so they determined to go to Ireland. They boarded a ship but it was hit by a terrible storm: three great waves swamped the vessel and half filled it with water. It is said that at this point the Lindisfarne Gospels were swept overboard and lost. The monks felt as if the world was against them. In great fear they abandoned the voyage and returned to the shores of the west coast. To have lost the Gospels was counted a very bad omen indeed. That night one of the bearers of the coffin, Hunred, had a dream in which Cuthbert came to him and told him that the Gospels would be found unharmed washed up on the sands near Whithorn in Galloway. So there the 'Congregation of St Cuthbert' or 'Cuthbert's Folk', as they were now called, went, to the place of St Ninian, the first saint known by name in the land beyond the Roman Wall.

Whenever there was a rumour of a Viking attack Cuthbert's folk would pack all their belongings and move again. They managed to travel the length and breadth of Northumbria without being captured. Obviously this was often due to the devotion and help of others. Wherever they went they were met by the faithful. They were given gifts of gold, fine garments and even land. Some time during this period of journeying the Vikings began to be colonisers rather than invaders. A more settled time was coming, there was intermarriage and some Vikings were becoming Christian. So Cuthbert's folk took courage and entered the Viking heartland of Yorkshire. They settled at Crayke only a few miles from York itself. While they were there a strange event occurred. When King Halfdan died in 882, Cuthbert appeared to the abbot in a dream and instructed him to seek out a captive Viking Christian called Guthfrith and make him King of Northumbria. In this way Guthfrith became king, in a ceremony that was a strange mixture of pagan and Christian actions and rites, oaths being sworn over the body of Cuthbert as well as over armlets and rings.

In thanksgiving Guthfrith gave the Cuthbert folk the old Roman fort at Chester-le-Street and there had a fine new church built for them. Here he endowed the shrine of Cuthbert with many rich gifts. Once settled in and knowing that things were going well, the monks gained a new courage. The abbot went to the king and said that just as Cuthbert had gained the king's freedom for him, so now Cuthbert had said that all the land between the Tyne and the Wear should be given to the monastery as part of its endowments. We do not know the king's reaction, but we do know that he endowed the church with this land. It is strange that Cuthbert, who lived so simply and sought to possess nothing, seemed to be guiding the brethren to take over great tracts of land! The little community from Lindisfarne was getting involved in political intrigue, determined to build up their landed wealth. At the same time Guthfrith knew that having the saint in his domain would bring great prestige and much wealth to the area. All this seems far removed from the hermit who lived on onions and wanted to be buried on the Farne.

Still, the Cuthbert cult spread throughout the land. From far and wide they came to the coffin-reliquary. In 934 the grandson of Alfred the Great, King Athelstan of Wessex, on his way to drive the Vikings out of York, came to the shrine. The Viking king had taken the lands that Guthfrith had given to the church at Chester-le-Street and shared

them with his own men. So 'Cuthbert' proved a good patriotic rallying point. Athelstan came bearing gifts – church silver and gold, valuable vestments including a priest's stole and maniple in gold and silk threads, and a copy of Bede's life of Cuthbert. He also gave a royal estate at Wearmouth. He then went on to a successful battle, and his visit to the shrine was well rewarded, for he became recognised as the King of all England.

The following years were good ones for the Cuthbert Folk, and life at Chester-le-Street seemed settled. But in 995 there was a Viking uprising and once more the Cuthbert folk were on the move.

A SURE SHELTER

You are our shelter, O Lord,
A shield in the battle,
A protection from the evil one.

You are our shelter, O Lord,
A haven from the high wave,
A harbour in the storm.

You are our shelter, O Lord,
A cover from the heat,
A guard against the icy blast.

You are our shelter, O Lord,
A light upon our path,
A Presence in our darkness.

You are our shelter, O Lord,
A companion in our travels,
There at the journey's end.

You are our shelter, O Lord.

118

17

Durham

THE journey from Chester-le-Street went close to where Cuthbert and his horse had been refreshed in the tumbledown bothy. Then it went on to more familiar ground as they travelled to Ripon. The last time Cuthbert had been there he still had his Celtic tonsure. This time his stay was even shorter than the last. The Cuthbert Folk stayed at Ripon for only four months. By then it seemed that the uprising was over and a new peace was coming to the area. It was time to return to Chester-le-Street. But they were not destined to do so. The company of monks was no longer a small travelling band, but had swollen to about five hundred in number. At some point as they neared the Chester-le-Street area the shrine-carrying carriage became firmly embedded in the mud. It really seemed unable and unwilling to move. For those who were not very sure what they should be doing, this was taken as a sign. 'Cuthbert does not want us to go to Chester-le-Street.' There were others who were more sure of where they wanted to go, and this message pleased them all. The return to Chester-le-Street was set about with so many problems. They needed a new place for the new world that was taking shape around them. There can be little doubt that some of the brethren knew of the island-like hill of Dunholm. Here the River Wear makes a great U-shape around an almost impregnable little plateau. The banks on all sides are steep. It would make a good place for a fortress, or for a beacon on a hill.

The bishop commanded that the great travelling company should stay where they were, and spend their time in fasting and prayer, that they might get some indication of where they should go next. Towards

the end of this time a monk named Eadmer said that he had received a vision and that Cuthbert wanted them to go to Dunholm. Almost as soon as this was mentioned it was discovered that the carriage with coffin and relics could be moved without much effort. But now where was this place Cuthbert wanted to rest? As they were not sure of the direction they were delighted to see ahead of them two women. One was calling to the other, 'Have you seen my dun cow? It has gone missing.' The other replied, 'Aye, I have seen it, it is at Dunholm – I'll show you where I mean.' Once again everyone was satisfied, those who did not know where to go and those who had an idea. All of the monks decided to follow the women. It was a strange procession, with a woman at the front calling her cow, a bishop and monks and the holy relics of Cuthbert and other saints following. The last part of the journey was again difficult, for the place was thick with trees and thorn bushes. Yet on the top of the near island there was a grass-covered plateau where the dun cow was grazing.

This was to be the new home for the Cuthbert Folk. The bishop ordered prayers of thanksgiving to be said immediately. Amongst those prayers was one for the blessing of this land and for its future church. There on the high plateau they quickly built a shelter for the shrine. Once again Cuthbert was under a temporary residence made up of branches and twigs interwoven. It was a little like the old days on the high moors. Then as soon as possible a wooden church was erected and dedicated. This held the shrine now, and it was not unlike the church that used to be on Lindisfarne. They now proceeded to build a more permanent home for the shrine. Three years after arriving at Dunholm, on September 4th, 998, there was a great red-letter day: the stone church was ready enough, the shrine was prepared – Cuthbert could rest at last. Pilgrims again thronged the resting-place of Cuthbert, though the actual building work on the church was not completed until 1017.

In the year 1066 there was yet more turmoil with the Norman invasion. The years that followed were horrific. William the Conqueror systematically began to lay waste the northern terrorities. In the winter of 1069, the last Saxon bishop of Durham, Ethelwine, fled before the Norman army and took the relics of Cuthbert with him for safe keeping. He went northwards away from the advancing army. That winter he went to Lindisfarne – it would seem that Cuthbert was to be forever going around his old diocese. However when the spring came, the dangers seemed to have passed away. Now once again Cuthbert and his folk had to wait for the tide to turn. There was a procession across the sands, as Cuthbert left Lindisfarne for the last time. From the simplicity of the island he returned to the shrine at Durham and all its growing splendour.

In 1093 the foundation stone of the huge cathedral of Durham was laid. It would rear up to be seen for miles around, and without any doubt is one of the greatest buildings in the world. In 1104, Cuthbert's relics were translated to the shrine behind the high altar. August 29th was the day fixed for the translation, but first it was decided that the prior and nine of the brothers should open the coffin and examine the body.

Because of the very nature of the veneration in which Cuthbert was held, this could not be done lightly. Deep and awe-filled were the prayers of the chosen ones and of the community. Their thoughts and fears swung between their own presumption that they should be checking on Cuthbert and the miracle of his body and the possibility that all inside the coffin had now turned to dust. They wrenched the lid off the coffin amidst fears and prayers, to discover inside yet another coffin, covered with a coarse linen cloth. This coffin was wonderfully carved and with runic writing. There was no doubt that this was the same wooden coffin that Eadbert had prepared for Cuthbert in the year of his elevation at Holy Island. Once again the monks hesitated before the relics of a saint and deep mysteries. Leofwin, a monk of great devotion, encouraged them and said how he thought they should proceed. They moved the coffin from behind the altar to the middle of the choir, where there was more room. There was another lid to remove. But it had iron rings at each end and was raised easily. On lifting the linen cloth inside they were aware of a sweet and pleasant smell. Cuthbert was lying on his side as if asleep. The whole of the group were overcome, tears flowed from their eyes and they repeatedly made the sign of the cross. They then prostrated themselves on the floor and recited together the seven penitential psalms. Then without getting up from their knees they approached the coffin once more. Now they discovered the other holy relics, and decided to remove these bones, but they could not do so without first lifting Cuthbert. So they lifted the body out, noticing how supple it was, like someone relaxed rather than dead. As evening and darkness was approaching they hurriedly replaced the body and returned it to its place behind the altar. The next day at the request of their abbot they returned, removed the body and examined all the other things in the coffin. The ivory comb, the shears, the silver altar, the chalice and paten were all there.

The following day a great company assembled for the ceremony of the saint's translation. Abbots, bishops, dignitaries from all over England and the continent were assembled. News spread quickly that Cuthbert had been discovered uncorrupt. One abbot in particular refused to believe it. He suggested that the monks of Durham were out to capture the populace by their stories, and maintained that others from outside the monastery should have witnessed this event to give it credence. A bitter battle was in danger of arising between opposing views. It was settled by the Abbot of Séez in Normandy, who persuaded the monks that he himself and a goodly company be allowed to investigate for themselves. Once more Cuthbert was brought out and lifted out of his coffin. The Abbot of Séez alone touched the corpse but he moved limbs, worked joints and bent the neck, raising the body in almost an upright position. Even the doubting abbot had to admit to the miracle.

Now a triumphant *Te Deum* was sung and the coffin closed once more. As it was carried out in the open the crowd surged around so much that the bearers could hardly move forward. The sermon by the bishop which was terribly long was mercifully cut short by a torrent of rain. The coffin was hurriedly returned to the cathedral. When the solemn Mass ended, Cuthbert was laid to rest behind the high altar.

Before the dissolution of the monasteries, in 1537, Cuthbert's shrine was visited by three royal commissioners. They were amazed at all the

treasures the shrine contained, and proceeded to annex the jewels and precious gifts for the crown. No doubt this included the Lindisfarne Gospels. Expecting to find more gifts in the coffin they had it forced open. Inside the carved wooden chest was Cuthbert lying on his side. The garments wrapping his body were still intact. The commissioners were so taken aback that they ordered the body to be kept in the vestry until it was discovered what the king would have them do with it. At his request it was buried again by the prior and monks in the shrine behind the high altar. Cuthbert was once more put to rest with prayers and devotions.

In 1827 the grave was opened again, this time in the presence of two prebendaries, the librarian and thirteen others. By now the wooden coffin had fragmented and was in a state of decay. In the tomb was still the portable altar, a beautiful pectoral cross, the silk and gold stole and maniple and the comb. All these were removed along with the pieces of the coffin. The body had now decayed and so at long last Cuthbert was allowed to rest. The mortal remains of the saint who became a fire in the north are under the slab that says

CUTHBERTUS.

Almighty God, who called Cuthbert out of the darkness of night to be the Fire of the North, set our hearts on fire with your love, and help us to show forth your light today, through Christ our Lord, who is the Light of the world and lives and reigns with you and the Holy Spirit, one God now and forever. AMEN

Bibliography

BERTRAM COLGRAVE (trans), *Two Lives of Saint Cuthbert* (Cambridge 1985).

BEDE, *A History of the English Church and People*, trans Leo Shirley-Price (Penguin Books 1955).

HILDA COLGRAVE, *Saint Cuthbert of Durham* (Northumberland Press 1947).

D. W. ROLLASON (ed), *Cuthbert Saint and Patron* (Dean and Chapter of Durham 1987).

ROSEMARY CRAMP, *The Background of Cuthbert's Life* (Durham Cathedral Lecture 1980).

C. F. BATTISCOMBE, *The Relics of Saint Cuthbert* (Oxford 1956).

C. J. STRANKS, *The Life and Death of Saint Cuthbert* (SPCK 1964).

JANET BACKHOUSE, *The Lindisfarne Gospels* (Phaidon 1981).

LUCY MENZIES, *Saint Columba of Iona* (Dent 1920).

PETER HUNTER BLAIR, *Northumbria in the Days of Bede* (Gollancz 1976).

J. F. WEBB and D. H. FARMER, *The Age of Bede* (Penguin 1983).

JOHN MARSDEN, *The Illustrated Bede* (Guild Publishing 1989).

JOHN MARSDEN, *Northanhymbre* (Kyle Cathie Ltd 1992).

Colum Kenny

POWER LINES
Celtic prayers about work

A series of modern prayers about work which incorporate the insights of the Celtic tradition. The book opens up Celtic patterns of prayer to focus on the work we all do in the presence of God.

——

BORDER LANDS
The best of David Adam

An SPCK hardback edition of selections from the first four of David Adam's books - an ideal introduction to Celtic spirituality.

——

(SPCK) and TRI/\NGLE Books
can be obtained from all good bookshops.
In case of difficulty,or for a complete list
of all our books,
contact:

**SPCK Mail Order
36 Steep Hill
Lincoln
LN2 1LU
(tel: 0522 527 486)**